The **NEW**
No Gimmick Diet

The *Buena Salud*® Guide to
Losing Weight and
Keeping It Off

The NEW
No Gimmick Diet

The *Buena Salud®* Guide to
Losing Weight and
Keeping It Off

❦

Jane L. Delgado, Ph.D., M.S.

Buena
Salud
Press

This book is published in the United States of America
First Edition
ISBN: 978-0-9979954-1-1
1 2 3 4 5 6 7 8 9 10

Library of Congress Control Number: 2016957216

This book is designed to provide accurate and authoritative information in regard to the subject matter covered. It is not intended to substitute for medical advice from a qualified health professional. The reader should consult his or her medical, health, or other competent professional before adopting any of the suggestions in this book or drawing inferences from it.

The author and the publisher specifically disclaim all responsibility for any liability, loss, or risk, personal or otherwise, that is incurred as a consequence, directly or indirectly, of the use and application of any of the contents of this book.

Table of Contents

INTRODUCTION

When I had lost nearly forty pounds, I realized that I had finally brought together all the science and experiences to manage my weight. My goal is to share with everyone what I learned and to put to rest the abundant bad advice that I had been given over the years.

I know how tough it is to maintain a healthy size because I have lived that challenge every day of my life. In the past, when I followed the advice of experts, I became very frustrated. As a psychologist and as someone who reads a lot of science, I found that the information that was available on getting to a healthy size ranged from useless to dangerous.

There were, of course, many testimonials and countless programs with catchy phrases. With their before-and-after pictures, the dramatic weight loss programs were enticing. All this was supported by anecdotes about how you could lose many pounds in a just a few days or weeks. Of course, each program emphasized how easy it would be to lose weight if you just followed their special plan, bought their special products, or signed up for their special offer. And, because we are human and tend to be hopeful, each easy solution is very, very seductive. By preying on those of us who were willing to try anything, the weight loss business has become a $59 billion dollar industry.[1]

For many of us, it seemed that if gaining the pounds happened so quickly and naturally, that there should be an equally fast, painless, and easy way to take them off. After trying countless ways to lose weight, we all learned that, sadly, it doesn't work that way. If weight loss were fast and easy, none of us would carry excess weight; we would all be at our healthy weight.

The truth about getting healthier is that it is tough. That is not what most people want to hear. In fact, you will not lose your weight either quickly or easily. To get to a healthy weight and to maintain that healthy weight takes work. A lot of work, time, and patience. After all these years, I have consolidated the most recent research and everything I have learned to help each one of us reach and maintain a healthy weight. The work we each have to do involves developing some new practices and discarding some old ones.

I can remember being concerned about my weight as far back as the fourth grade. Finding clothes that fit was also challenging. A few stores had a "chubby section," but I did not feel good about what I saw when I shopped there. The clothes were not as much fun as those my friends could buy. Even more discouraging was the fact that the choices on display gave a second meaning to wearing coveralls.

Fortunately, I had a wonderful mother who instilled in me a healthy measure of self-esteem that gave me a positive self-image regardless of my size. I was blessed, because even though I was told I had excess weight, I still felt good about myself. Sadly, for many young girls and increasingly, for young boys, that is not the case. They are often the ones who are bullied and who bear the brunt of cruel and esteem-damaging jokes.

While my mother nurtured my self-esteem, the cultural norms were not as supportive. Culture can be cruel, and the message was very clear: according to the charts, based on my height and weight I was far from where I should be. Since I knew I was not going to get any taller, the ideal weight specified for someone of my height in all those charts seemed more of a barrier than an achievable goal. But that did not stop me from trying. As a result, I tracked my weight for decades. I tried whatever plan or program was recommended in order to reach what was deemed the ideal weight for someone of my height.

During all those years, I had to contend with all the pronouncements of experts who had never really had to manage their own weight. Their words detailed all the things I did that were wrong. They also pointed to aspects of my personal behavior that were problematic. Depending on which expert was currently fashionable, the reason I did not lose weight was either that I lacked willpower, that I was lazy, or that I ate foods that were bad for me.

Even with all that negativity, I still tried every new weight loss plan in the hope that one would work. Although I would have limited success, I would consistently gain the weight back over time. I probably lost and gained enough weight over the years to make up several people.

I was not alone in my efforts. I commiserated with my friends as we tried the program of the moment. A few of them lost weight, but most of us did the boomerang— losing some weight and then gaining it back, plus a little extra.

I tried it all. I joined gyms, adding every type of spot exercise to no avail, and methodically wrote down my exercises until it all became meaningless. The activities of my regular life seemed to crowd out the best-intentioned exercise plan. (One friend tried to make light of her results, observing wryly that on the thirty-day diet, the only thing she lost was five days.)

When I read that the average person gains one to two pounds every year after age 35, I calculated that by the time I was in my fifties I could conceivably have added a lot of weight to my 5' 3" frame. As the years passed, I logged my weight and watched the pounds increase. It seemed inevitable, and I accepted my plus size as part of my life.

Since I was involved in health and wellness, I decided to try to be as healthy as I could be regardless of my size. I ate healthy foods, followed a low-sodium diet, avoided carbonated drinks, and tried to exercise as much as possible to manage my weight. Most important of all, I was very respectful of everyone, especially those who were making a great effort to manage their weight as well as those who had given up. I had been in both situations.

I still gained weight. At times I felt that all I had to do was look at food, and the pounds would pile on. More discouraging still, even when I was successful on a diet, eventually, over time, the pounds would come back and stay.

Since my size would fluctuate, my closet reflected a range of sizes and styles that fit wherever I happened to be on the scale. Fortunately, clothing manufacturers had finally realized that there were people who needed larger sizes and did not want to just wear caftans. I was okay with shopping in the plus-size department for attractive clothes because I realized clothes that fit and were not flowing were the most flattering. My friends knew that regardless of my size, whenever I went swimming I wore a black two-piece bikini. I may have been larger than other people, but frankly, I felt as sexy as ever.

While I may have looked good and felt good about myself, as I got older, injuries from my teenage and more athletic years began to create problems that I had not anticipated. My knees would hurt and I could not walk as far as I wanted to. I learned that every pound of excess weight added four pounds of load to my knees and increased wear and tear on my knee joints. I wanted to lose weight not because of my clothing size but to avoid the pain in my knees. Yet my efforts seemed futile: I could still not lose a significant amount of weight. Then, all of sudden, a new impetus to work on my size came to me from an unexpected source.

One day my BFF shared with me that she had met the love of her life. They were going to get married in a few months. I knew I would definitely be there to celebrate their union. But I also knew that the cost of the airfare and hotel for my husband and me would put a serious dent in our budget. We could afford to go to the wedding, but there was not going to be room in the budget for a new dress. I would have to make do with what was in my closet.

I looked in the back of my closet where I stored my "someday" dresses and rediscovered a dress I had worn only once. Just seven years before, I had poured myself into that dress and looked absolutely adorable. I knew that if I lost 10 pounds, the dress would fit again.

As someone who had lost weight many, many times, I knew that it would be hard but possible for me to lose 10 pounds before my friend's wedding. I weighed 237 pounds. Ten pounds (four percent of my body weight) did not seem like a lot of weight to lose.

When I was younger, I could lose that amount in a few weeks. It would be tougher now, since, as I had learned from experience, the older I was the harder it became to lose each pound. Still, I knew I would do it because I knew the basics: "eat less and move more." Much to my dismay, it became apparent after a while that this core strategy was not working. I was going to have to do something different. So I did.

I began by looking into the assorted options that always come up in discussions about eating less. For many reasons, surgery was not an option that I was interested in considering. And while there are medicines that may be helpful, I knew they were not the answer for me. Moreover, I knew to avoid the many dietary supplements that are advertised and promoted aggressively in the media. Dietary supplements are not regulated as medicines, and weight loss products had been taken off the shelves too many times for my comfort. Laxatives, diuretics, and similar compounds were totally unappealing. Most importantly, using these products is not sustainable as a life-long strategy, since some of them may actually do more harm than good in the long run. I wanted to get to a healthier size without putting myself at increased risk for other health problems.

What needed to change had to involve more than food and activity. I had to change my approach to when and how I would eat. I realized that just knowing that something is good for you or is a solution is not enough to cause a change in behavior. You need to accept the knowledge in your head and in your heart. And acceptance would mean thinking about eating in a different way. But what was I supposed to do? The suggestions of many well-meaning experts seemed to point me toward the same loop that had taken me nowhere.

What still seemed to echo in my head were the words of a French nutrition expert that I had heard years before. During a roundtable on healthy eating, Dr. France Bellisle had commented that *"the French concept of hunger is different than the American concept."* I had filed away her statement as provocative and kept it in my mind. Her words helped show me how to unlock the part of what I had to do that was new and radically different.

I have to admit that her explanation of how to approach food initially seemed odd and unreasonable. At the same time, I wondered what would happen if I were to take her words and act on them. I would have to think about eating in a radically different way. I would have to develop a set of new practices to avoid all the drivers to eat (both internally and externally) and change most of what I had been doing throughout my life. Since nothing else had worked, I figured I had nothing to lose but the few pounds that I wanted to lose anyway. And so I followed her advice. I began to reflect on how I felt when I was hungry and what I did. I also began a mental calibration of the different degrees of hunger and to recognize that there were many triggers to make me eat more than I should and even when I was not hungry.

By the day of the wedding, I had lost the 10 pounds. I fit into my dress and put on my matching gold sandals. My husband and I danced all night. Much to my surprise, my knees did not hurt. Even though my dress was still a little snug, I felt great.

I thought about what I had accomplished, and I was thrilled. The ten-pound weight loss was the result of applying and recasting everything I had learned over the decades about what makes us do what we do. I was so pleased with my success that I began to think that maybe I could continue on the same path.

I wondered if I could actually lose more weight if I just kept doing what I had been doing. I would focus on thinking in the new way and just make my new practices my way of life. I had done it for the past few months. Maybe I could do it for a few more months to see if there were even more changes. So I decided to continue on my program and see if I could lose more of my excess weight. I knew that the challenges would be huge, since Thanksgiving and the holidays were just two months away.

To my amazement, in eight months I lost a total of 32 pounds. Three months later, I had lost an additional five pounds. I had lost 37 pounds in less than a year. Although I didn't notice a huge difference when I looked in the mirror, I felt much better, and I found that my clothes were starting to fit in a different way.

After 15 months I, had lost 42 pounds. The pounds I had accumulated, lost, and regained over the past twenty years were gone. The insights I gained, ongoing developments in science, and the many people who have shared experiences and tips about what worked and did not work for them are what inspired me to write this book.

This book is not for everybody, but it is for all of us who carry some excess weight, who are hoping to find a way to get the results we want to achieve, and who want to keep the weight off. While I needed to lose some excess weight, there are others who need to gain weight.

The overall goal must be to be healthier. Weight is just one of the measures that you track along the way. The challenge is for each person to set a reasonable target weight, keeping in mind that weight is only *one* measure of how healthy you are, and then to maintain that healthy weight and all of your other healthy behaviors.

Setting goals is a process, and one key is for those goals to be attainable. Once the first goal is achieved, another goal, such as an another reasonable target weight, can be set. This way each person achieves small successes. Those successes will turn into added motivation to continue the life change in progress.

I knew that for me, getting my weight down to about 200 pounds would be a major accomplishment. Granted, I would still be heavier than recommended for most people my height, but it would be a dramatic change for me. By keeping my target of about two hundred in the forefront, I made it. I know there are those who will criticize my goal and point out that I am still in the obese range. But for me, this is fabulous progress, and I am healthier for having achieved it. And after all, this is my journey.

Keep in mind that the goal is different for each of us. Being healthy and fit can mean different things depending on your gender, race, ethnicity, age, height, body type, and all the other factors that circumscribe your life. Before you begin any plan, you should see your health care provider to get a baseline of where you are. You also need to get an all-clear on your plans to fine-tune your size and overhaul your relationship with food. Just as we know that one size does not fit all, or even most, the practices and approaches you develop must be tailored to you so that you can incorporate each one into your daily life.

What I actually did to change my approach to eating and lose the weight is based on what I learned from decades of research on food, nutrition, and metabolism; listening to those who cared for people who want to lose weight; and on my own experiences as a clinician. Learning vital new approaches to how, what, and when I ate changed everything.

Again, no single plan enables everyone to lose weight and keep it off. That is why this book provides key information rather than on a specific plan. The latest research on weight and BMI and what they actually measure can help you set reasonable goals and expectations. The discussion of hunger and what it means is key to helping you recalibrate feeling full and feeling hungry, because an important part of getting to a healthy size is knowing how you respond to all sorts of cues around you and within yourself.

By knowing the many factors that drive how we eat, what we eat, and when we eat, we can learn to master them. While culture and advertising are often thought of as aspects of our life that mold and define how and what we eat, the imperative is for each one of us to examine the cues around us that drive us to eat more than we need to eat and make it difficult to make the best choices about when we eat or to eat food in healthy amounts. There are real obstacles that we must learn to handle and longstanding behaviors that we have to unlearn.

If you have worked to manage your size throughout your life, you know there are many plans and programs. You also know that most of them do not work over the long run. Like most of us, I have tried many approaches to managing my size. Both science and our shared experience make it clear that there is no single magic solution. The approach in this book includes an array of healthy practices and insights for changing your approach to food that will make all the difference. For example, if you are aware of how different aspects of our culture drive us to eat, you can choose to create a support system that will allow you to eat in the way which works for you.

I present the latest findings to help you use this information to develop and adopt new practices to make you successful in changing how you eat. I focus on the best practices you need to know, so that you can adapt them to your way of life. And a best practice needs to be practiced. You may not get it right the first time or do it all the time, but the more you practice, the more it become a part of your life.

In conversations with so many people about getting to a healthier weight, it is evident that most people can repeat the facts, knowledge, and everything you need to know about how to eat healthy and manage your weight. The practices and strategies you choose to put in place will help you on your journey. You can succeed.

The essential message of this book is that the best plan for you must be custom-made for you and by you. While there are many professionals who can give you advice about what to eat and how to exercise, you need to own this as your journey.

I want to help you on your journey to better health through managing your size. This is a life-long challenge for me, and I will keep you up- to-date on what is working and what is not working. Let me know what works for you by sharing your experiences on janeonhealth.blogspot.com. We can learn from each other along the way.

---

[1]   *The U.S. Weight Loss Market: 2014 Status Report & Forecast.* Bharat Book Bureau. Mumbai

CHAPTER 1
It Is Your Journey

If you are reading this book, you know what you want— you want to be a healthier size. While there is no single plan that will work for everybody, the information, best practices, and strategies in this book provide tools that you can use to get to where you want to be. Being healthier is a lifelong journey that you need to define for yourself. At different points in your life, you will have to recalibrate based on how you are doing. Sometimes you will have to sharpen your tools, drop some, or pick up new tools. I am glad to share with you an assortment of tools and strategies that can work for you.

We know that losing weight is difficult and that the more weight you have to lose to be in the "normal" range the more *unlikely* it is that you will lose it.[2] Dr. Alison Fildes of the Department of Primary Care and Public Health Sciences, King's College London, and her team analyzed the records of 76,704 obese men and 99,791

1

obese women over a nine-year period. Most of the people were unable either to reach normal weight or maintain their weight loss. According to their results, "the annual probability of achieving a five percent weight reduction was one in eight for men and one in seven for women with morbid obesity."

One of the most important aspects of your health journey is to allow yourself to make stops along the way and decide whether you want to continue. You may feel that where you are is good enough, or you may decide to go a little farther down your path. The key to a healthier you is to be reasonable about what you set out to do. You need to focus on what you will be able to do.

It Is Not About Willpower

Alice has always struggled with her weight. When she asked me how I lost my weight, I told her everything that I had done and how I had changed the way I thought about being hungry. Her response was to dismiss what I said with, "You just have willpower. That's what it is all about." And I said, "No. Managing your weight is not about willpower. I have always had willpower, but I could not get to the size I knew would be healthier for me."

The definition of "willpower" in *The Free Dictionary* is (1) the ability to control oneself and determine one's actions; (2) firmness of will.[3] In our society, willpower is a key concept, because we are strong believers in self-determination, with willpower being its natural expression. Embedded in our way of life is the expectation that you can do whatever you want to do if you want it badly enough. For Spanish-speaking people, the term *ganas* implies this kind of desire. To have *ganas* means that you truly want something and that you will do what it takes to make it happen.

What I heard from many is that while willpower may be a useful construct for some behaviors when it comes to eating healthy, all it does is discourage those who want to lose weight. Rather than being supportive, the underside of saying that managing your weight is about willpower is the not-so-subtle implication that those who struggle to maintain a healthy size lack willpower and are gluttons who cannot control their eating. The problem with that train of thought is that it diminishes the reality of the drivers in our culture. These sometimes- subtle drivers push us to eat regardless of our level of fullness and teach us to satisfy all feelings of hunger immediately with whatever food is fast to get and easy to consume.

That is why, when it comes to healthy eating, the notion of willpower is not only inaccurate but actually undermining to the very people we are trying to support as they manage their weight. So to the concept of willpower I say "phooey." I know lots of men and women with willpower who nevertheless struggle to manage their weight. What we need to do is develop strategies that help us. We need to add some new approaches that are helpful and let go of the ones that do not help. It is not about what someone else wants you to do or what is a goal for someone else. It is all about you.

Each person has to define the path they want to take and then identify and gather the tools and strategies that will work for them. A critical first step is to let go of all the negative societal attitudes about excess weight. We all know that there is tremendous social pressure to be a certain size and shape.

Also, whether you recognize it or not, social stigma has many negative consequences that are part of the challenge in getting healthier. Issues of weight bias[4] are real and damaging.

According to Dr. Reginald Washington, Chief Medical Officer, Rocky Mountain Hospital for Children in Denver, Colorado, weight bias "can be defined as the inclination to form unreasonable judgments based on a person's weight." He cautions all of us that as part of "an effort to avoid weight bias, new efforts to reduce obesity must be evaluated to determine whether these efforts do, in fact, add to the problem."

Researchers have warned that "stigmatization of obese individuals threatens health, generates health disparities, and interferes with effective obesity intervention efforts."[5] That is why you need to put negative feelings about your size behind you *before* you set your targets.

Your overall goal is to be healthier and to recognize that changes in your appearance are only a side effect. While looking good is nice, feeling good is essential.

The key belief you must embrace is that the journey toward better health is your journey, and a target weight is the first stopping point. Given all the data, a good place to begin is to better understand the meaning of weight. While it is one measure that you can use to track your progress, in order to better plan your journey toward a healthier life, you need to understand what weight really is.

Weight

Technically, weight is the measure of how much force is pushing down on you as a result of gravity. Most of us have a good idea of what we weigh now, what we have weighed at other points in our life, and what we would like our weight to be.

The topic of weight and what is someone's ideal weight is the subject of many discussions. Everyone tries to comment on what someone should weigh. According to the National Heart, Lung, and Blood Institute (NHLBI) your height and weight are key measures that can be used to calculate your body mass index (BMI). There are many online calculators to determine your BMI. BMI is a value that has been found to correlate with other measures of total fat in your body.[6] There are various ways to calculate BMI, but most people use the NHLBI descriptions below:

NHLBI Description	BMI
Underweight	<18.5
Normal	18.5 - 24.9
Overweight	25.0 - 29.9
Obesity (Class I)	30.0 - 34.9
Obesity (Class II)	35.0 - 39.9
Obesity (Class III)	40.0 +

Although BMI has been used since the nineteenth century,[7] it is not as accurate as you may think. For example, BMI tables overestimate obesity in athletes and people with a muscular build, and underestimate obesity in older persons or people who have lost some of their muscles. It also does not take into account differences due to a person's age, gender, body type, race, ethnicity, or a combination of these factors. And research into BMI has revealed some results that came as a big surprise to me.

What seems like a small weight loss makes a huge difference in your health. When many of us think about getting to a healthier weight, we think about losing many pounds. While that may be a long term goal, research shows that a five percent weight loss decreases the fat in the middle area of the body and helps to increase the responsiveness of many of the organs in the body to insulin.[8] As weight loss increases, it starts to change the way the fat tissue in the body functions. This is what a weight loss of five percent means for people of different starting weights:

Your Weight (lbs.)	5% Loss
300	15 lbs.
275	13.75 lbs.
250	12.5 lbs.
225	11.25 lbs.
200	10 lbs.
175	8.5 lbs.
150	7.5 lbs.

Normal weight is not best. Looking at the results from national studies, the National Center for Health Statistics (NCHS) identified some unexpected trends. In order to better understand the outcomes of varying levels of BMI, the NCHS tried to make sense of existing data. Researchers used the measure of excess death to see the impact of BMI on a person's lifespan. Excess death is a measure that indicates how many more people would die from a specific factor compared to the number that would have died anyway.

They documented that having a body mass index (BMI) in the overweight range resulted in *fewer* excess deaths than among persons who were normal weight.[9] The groups who had more excess deaths were people who were underweight and those with BMIs over 35. In her more recent research, Dr. Katherine Flegal, a leading and prolific researcher at the National Center for Health Statistics, looked only at data for people whose weight was normal weight or above normal. Based on even more data, she found that people with a BMI over 35 (Class II obesity) had more mortality from all causes, but that being "overweight [BMI under 30] was associated with significantly lower all-cause mortality."[10]

This was confusing to some, and it left unanswered questions about the health impact on a person as BMI increased. In 2014, Dr. Cari Kitahara an investigator at the NIH, National Cancer Institute, Division of Cancer Epidemiology & Genetics and her associates[11] published the findings from their extensive analysis of twenty studies. In this review they looked at 304,000 people of normal weight and 9,500 people with Class III obesity.

The people in the studies lived in the United States, Sweden, and Australia. What they found was that as BMI went up, so did the years of life lost.

BMI	Years of Life Lost
40 - 44.9	6.5
45 - 49.9	8.9
50 - 54.9	9.8
55 - 59.9	13.7

But what does all this research mean? Does it mean that it's okay, or even desirable, to be overweight? If the population is roughly one-third underweight or normal, one-third overweight, and one-third obese, how could this change how people see themselves or the goals that people should set?

Why did the countless press releases about the dangers of obesity seem to overlook the news that being overweight is okay, but that more excess weight leads to worse health outcomes? This information is key to understanding why it is essential to manage our weight and to set meaningful goals. It may also be more motivating for people to know that they may not have to lose as much weight as they thought, and that being too thin is also not good. It also leaves unanswered the question of what should be the focus of our efforts to be healthier.

While BMI is relatively easy to calculate, its main importance is how it correlates with body fat. There are some key facts to understand about body fat: what it is, where in our body it is located, and what risk factors can compromise the health of people who have too much of it.

About Body Fat. For a long time, people were taught that the fat cells in our bodies were just globs of excess white matter. However, that is wrong. We now know that a fat cell is part of our endocrine system. The endocrine system is the part of our body that produces all the hormones that we need to function. These hormones control everything from sleep to sexual function to metabolism. Some researchers have even said that fat is an endocrine organ.[12] We know that fat cells produce leptin, a hormone that works to suppress hunger and increase metabolism. Although people with more fat cells have more leptin, some investigators have proposed that people with excess weight have built up a resistance to the signals leptin sends to the body. Some research also suggests a relationship between leptin and ghrelin (the "hunger hormone").

All fat is not the same. The two major kinds of fat are brown fat and white fat. The white fat stores energy, while the brown fat burns it. While brown fat makes up 5 percent of a baby's weight, the amount of brown fat in the body decreases over time. That is why the Division of Nutrition, Physical Activity, and Obesity at the Centers for Disease Control and Prevention (CDC) clarified that "children and teen's BMIs need to be age and sex-specific because the amount of body fat changes with age, and the amount of body fat differs between girls and boys."[13]

Adults have only small reserves of brown fat in their shoulders and neck. The important point is that fat has a key role with respect to the hormones in our body. The problem is that when we have too much fat, it becomes a burden on all of the systems in our body.

But actually measuring total body fat is complicated. So BMI is used to give a rough idea of how much fat a person has, even though we know that it is not accurate for many people. Also, when it comes to fat, the concerns are not just how much fat you have but where you carry your excess body fat.

The importance of your waist size is that it is an estimate of the fat in the middle of your body. Excess fat in your abdominal area surrounds your vital organs and threatens your health. Your body shape (apple or pear-shaped) is often used as an indicator of how much fat you carry in your middle area. That is why knowing your waist size is another way to estimate where you may have excess fat.

As we learned more about body fat, the research suggested that women with a waist over 35 inches and men with a waist over 40 inches had a higher risk for heart disease and diabetes. Much to my surprise, this measurement of waist size is not the same as your belt or pant size. According to the NHLBI, the correct way to measure your waist is to "stand and place a tape measure around your middle, just above your hipbones. Measure your waist just after you breathe out."[14] When I measured myself using this method, my waist was larger than I had thought.

The concern about your waist, sometimes referred to as central obesity, should raise a red flag for many of us. Recent research suggests that people who have normal weight *and* have large waists do much worse in the long term than other people who do not have a large waist regardless of whether the person was overweight or obese.[15]

Your health is even further compromised when you have more fat in your abdominal area and some or all of the following risk factors:

- ☀ high blood pressure (hypertension)
- ☀ high LDL cholesterol ("bad" cholesterol)

- low HDL cholesterol ("good" cholesterol)
- high triglycerides
- high blood glucose (sugar)
- family history of premature heart disease
- physical inactivity
- cigarette smoking

Better Than BMI. Given the limitations of BMI, there was a need to develop a better measure based on information from actual people. Knowing that your age, gender, height, weight, and waist circumference are all easily accessible pieces of information, Nir Y. Krakauer from the Department of Civil Engineering, The City College of New York in New York and Jesse C. Krakauer[16] of Middletown Medical in Middletown, New York developed " A Body Shape Index" (ABSI). This value is based on actual measurements of people in the United States and information on the ones who had died. They used the data from the 14,105 non-pregnant adults who participated in the National Health and Nutrition Examination Survey (NHANES) 1999– 2004.

The Krakauers state clearly that "ABSI correlation with mortality hazard held across the range of age, sex, and BMI, and for both white and black ethnicities (but not for Mexican ethnicity)." What the ABSI value provides is the likelihood that someone would die prematurely. A value of less than one meant the risk was less than that of the typical person, and a value of greater than one meant the risk was higher. I found the results from the online calculator to be very informative.

What was incredibly informative was their statement that "we found that both low and high BMI increased the mortality hazard...The lowest mortality hazard was for the middle quintile of both BMI and WC [waist circumference], although the population median was in the World Health Organization (WHO) 'overweight' or 'pre-obese' category." Once again, being overweight had the best health outcome. This was very helpful to me when it came time to set goals and keep track of my weight.

Starting your journey

I was talking to my friend Olivia about how my book was a rational approach to losing weight and how, according to the CDC, people who are overweight but not obese actually live longer than persons who are normal weight. I emphasized that the right weight for each person cannot be determined by just looking at a chart. Olivia seemed surprised and confused. She then asked, "Well then, how does a person know how much they should weigh?" I responded, "The goal should be based on a series of choices and decisions that a person makes." My answer made her brow furrow. It was not the simple answer she was looking for.

Your target goals need to be tailored to you. At the same time, your timeline has to be realistic: you have to give yourself time to get to a healthier place, and once there you have to give your body time to settle into its new shape. You will decide how much you do to improve your health and when you will stop.

As you begin your journey to a healthier you, it is important to set your first goal. This goal should be based on a realistic sense of what you can accomplish over the next few months. While it may be helpful to track your weight, it is good to set other goals for yourself so that you can know how you are doing.

Understanding the impact of your weight and waist on your health is key to setting reasonable targets. To be successfully met, we need some targets that are aspirational and others that we can feel reasonably sure we can achieve. In my case, I decided to target and track three aspects of my life to document my progress: weight, clothing, and overall health.

Weight. While weight may be easy to measure, it is very hard to set a reasonable weight target. Too often the targets we set are ambitious in both the amount of weight to lose and the timeframe. As a result, we set ourselves up for failure by making targets such as losing 10 pounds in a month or seeing how fast we can lose weight or who can lose the most in a certain time period. The evidence is that for most people, a weight loss of five to seven percent of body weight can have a positive impact on health. Although it may sound odd, reasonable expectations are better when it comes to successfully managing your weight. What does this mean?

Since I only had three months before my friend's wedding, I decided that a 4 percent weight loss would be a good target. When I reached my target, I was surprised at how much better I actually felt. And although I had planned to stop my journey at that point, I decided to see what would happen if I continued using the strategies that I had adopted and kept going. When I looked at the following numbers from the NHLBI online BMI calculator, I realized that it was unlikely that I would get to the normal or overweight range. Instead of being discouraged, I decided that Obesity Class I was a reasonable target. I did not have to get there but I would keep it as a reference point.

I had not weighed less than 200 pounds for over 20 years. But I decided that this was my journey and I would do what I could. I made the decision to continue

Weight (lbs.)	BMI	Percent lost	Category
237	42	0%	Obesity (Class III)
227	40.2	4%	Obesity (Class III)
217	38.4	8%	Obesity (Class II)
207	36.7	13%	Obesity (Class II)
197	34.9	17%	Obesity (Class I)
169	29.9	29%	Overweight
140	24.8	41%	Normal

with my new insights of embracing my mild hunger and see how far I would get. I would work to get under 197 pounds over the next year. And, given my history, I would consider an ending weight in the 200-pound range a success. The goal was to stay on track to being as healthy as I could be with the understanding that there would be setbacks and plateaus.

Clothing. Knowing how my clothes fit would be a rough indicator of how I was doing. I know how people who have different weights sometimes wear the same size, while other people who weigh the same may wear very different sizes. And one of my friends was so embarrassed about her size that she would cut the labels off her clothes so that no one would know what size she wore. Fortunately, I had learned early in life the lesson that you buy clothes because they fit and not because of the number on the size tag. It did not matter to me whether it was an 18W or a 22W.

Overall Health. It is one thing to say that you *will* feel better and another thing to *actually* feel better. By the time I reached my initial goal, I *felt* better. Although I knew that feeling better would be an eventual outcome, I did not realize just how much better I would really feel.

I had been getting increasingly worried about my mobility. It's not like I was ever a runner, but my knees hurt. I came to understand why knee replacement is so common among older persons in the United States. The wear and tear that ends up as osteoarthritis is a consequence of people trying to move regardless of their size. Over time, cartilage naturally wears down. Whether because of age, past injury, health conditions, or heredity, the knees are not as good as they once were. Ten pounds may not sound like a significant amount of weight, but to my knees it made a huge difference. I appreciated how much better they felt.

Feeling Better is the Goal. The challenge is not just to focus on your appearance or the pictures that are used to show the dramatic effects of some supplement or diet scheme. In my case, losing forty pounds did not have the dramatic effect on my appearance that might be expected. That would be discouraging for some people, but for me the weight loss was about being healthy and feeling better.

Since the goals are to improve overall heath and feel better, the important questions to ask are: How do you feel? What is your heart telling you? Can you do more of what you enjoy? What does your health care provider say about your overall health?

There are many considerations that go into creating your own journey. Before starting your journey, here is some key advice I would like to share with you:

1. See your health care provider before you start any healthy eating or exercise program.
2. Losing 10 to 15 pounds will make you feel better.
3. Losing a half-pound each week is very ambitious.
4. There will be weeks when your weight stays the same even though you're staying on your program. Sometimes it may take months before there is a change.
5. Reaching your goal weight is difficult. Staying there is even harder.
6. Your physical appearance may not change dramatically, but you will feel the changes as you are able to move around easier during your normal day.
7. Make sure to get the sleep you need. Research shows that sleep-deprived people gain weight.

8. What worked for you in the past may not be as helpful in the present.

To be successful, you have to make your new behaviors life-long practices that change based on your health and your experiences. Think of what you do to have healthy teeth. You have to work at it every day and go in for regular checkups. You may skip a day of flossing, but you will have to make up for it later. It is the same with managing your weight. You have to work at it every day in order to maintain your healthy body. Unlike your teeth, you cannot replace your entire body. Take care of what you have.

---

[2]   Fildes, A., Charlton, J., Rudisill, C., Littlejohns, P., Prevost, A. T. and Gulliford, M.C. "Probability of an Obese Person Attaining Normal Body Weight: Cohort Study Using Electronic Health Records," *American Journal of Public Health*. Published online ahead of print, July 16, 2015.

[3]   http://www.thefreedictionary.com/willpower. Accessed May 12, 2015.

[4]   Washington, R. L. "Childhood obesity: issues of weight bias," *Preventing Chronic Disease* 2011; 8(5):A94. http://www.cdc.gov/pcd/issues/2011/sep /10_0281.htm. Accessed July 15, 2015.

[5]   Puhl, R. M. and Heuer, C.A. "Obesity Stigma: Important Considerations for Public Health," *American Journal of Public Health*. June 2010, Vol. 100, No. 6, Pgs. 1019–1028.

[6]   Garrow, J.S. and Webster, J. "Quetelet's index (W/H2) as a measure of fatness," *International Journal of Obesity* 1985 Vol.9 Issue 2 Pgs.147-53.

[7]   Quetelet LAJ. *Physique sociale* 2, p. 92. Brussels: C. Muquardt, 1869.

[8]   Magkos, F.; Fraterrigo, G.; Yoshino, J.; Luecking, C.; Kirbach, K.; Kelly, S.C.; de las Fuentes, L.; He, S.: Okunade,A.L.; Patterson, B.W., and Klein, S. "Effects of Moderate and Subsequent Progressive Weight Loss on Metabolic Function and Adipose Tissue Biology in Humans with Obesity." *Cell Metabolism* 23, 1–1, April 12, 2016. DOI: http://dx.doi.org/10.1016/j.cmet.2016.02.005

[9]   Flegal, K. M. "Supplemental Analyses for Estimates of Excess Deaths Associated with Underweight, Overweight, and Obesity in the U.S. Population," NCHS Health E-Stat, January 7, 2010.

[10]   Flegal, K.M.; Kit, B.K.; Orpana, H. and Graubard, B. I. "Association of All-Cause Mortality with Overweight and Obesity Using Standard Body Mass Index Categories: A Systematic Review and Meta-analysis," *JAMA*, January 2, 2013, Vol. 309, No.1, Pgs.71-82.

[11]   Kitahara, C.M.; Flint, A.J.; Berrington de Gonzalez, A.; Bernstein, L.; Brotzman, M.; MacInnis, R.J.; Moore, S. C.; Robien, K.; Rosenberg, P. S.; Singh, P.N.; Weiderpass, E.; Adami, H.O.; Anton-Culver, H.; Ballard-Barbash, R.; Buring, J. E.; Freedman, D.M.; Fraser, G.E.; Beane Freeman, L. E.; Gapstur, S.M.; Gaziano, J. M.; Giles, G. G.; Håkansson, N.; Hoppin, J.A.; Hu, F. B.; Koenig, K.; Linet, M.S.; Park, Y.; Patel, A.V.; Purdue,

M. P.; Schairer, C.; Sesso, H.D.; Visvanathan, K.; White, E.; Wolk, A.; Zeleniuch-Jacquotte, A. and Hartge P. "Association between Class III Obesity (BMI of 40-59 kg/m2) and Mortality: A Pooled Analysis of 20 Prospective Studies," *PLoS Med.* 2014; 11(7): DOI: http://dx.doi.org/10.1371/journal.pmed.1001673.

[12]   Hutley, L. and Prins, J. B. "Fat as an Endocrine Organ: Relationship to the Metabolic Syndrome," *American Journal of the Medical Sciences.* December 2005, Vol. 330, Issue 6, Pgs. 280-9.

[13]   About Adult BMI." (May 15, 2015). Retrieved from http://www.cdc.gov/healthyweight/assessing/bmi/adult_bmi/index.html

[14]   National Heart, Lung, and Blood Institute (NHLBI). Accessed 07/25/15. http://www.nhlbi.nih.gov/health/educational/lose_wt/risk.htm

[15]   Sahakyan, K.R.; Somers, V.K.; Rodriguez-Escudero, J.P.; Hodge, D.O.; Carter, R.E.; Sochor, O.; Coutinho, T.; Jensen, M.D.; Roger, V.L.; Singh, P.; and, Lopez-Jimenez, F. "Normal-Weight Central Obesity: Implications for Total and Cardiovascular Mortality." *Annals of Internal Medicine.* November 10, 2015. DOI: http://dx.doi.org/10.7326/M14-2525

[16]   Krakauer, N. Y. and Krakauer, J. C. "A New Body Shape Index Predicts Mortality Hazard Independently of Body Mass Index," *PLoS ONE.* 7(7): July 18, 2012. Vol. 7, Issue 7, Pgs. 1-10. DOI: http://dx.doi.org/10.1371/journal.pone.0039504

CHAPTER 2
Feeling Hungry

I love the variety of foods at my local weekend farmer's market. The vegetables are from local farms, the cheeses are handmade a few hours away, and all the baked goods still have that fresh-out-of-the-oven smell. To add to all this wholesomeness, there are food stalls that carry a range of prepared foods including paella, crepes, and lamb bacon. Everything looks so tasty and good. The smells are total seduction.

I was born loving to eat. My mother said that even as an infant, I would smile and make sounds of pleasure as I ate. She would hear me go "mmmm" and know that I was enjoying my meal. I still like food, and I appreciate the fact that receiving nourishment is only one of the positive outcomes of the eating experience.

This means that I accept that I eat for many reasons, with nutrition being only one of them. What I learned is that being successful at managing your weight is all about learning new ways to experience the foods that we eat.

To begin with, we have to recognize that since food stimulates all of our senses, we need to focus on the interaction of our senses with what and how we eat. We should eat something because all of our senses become engaged—it looks appealing, the aroma is familiar, when we taste it we can savor the flavors, touching it is an almost primal experience, and hearing the crunch tells us it is fresh and delicious. All this adds to the yumminess of what we eat. In addition to the sensory experience it provides, food can evoke memories, both good and not so good.

There is no doubt that food engages every part of our brain. It is the variety of combinations of our senses and experiences that makes bacon yummy for one person, while absolutely repugnant to another. That is why each person has go-to comfort foods. For one person it may be canned tomato soup and a grilled cheese sandwich, while for another it may be hot chocolate. Our choice of favorite foods and drinks reflects more than the need for nutrition and hydration. Food stirs all sorts of senses and feelings. That is why when we try to manage our weight, we have to think about what we find appealing in food and what makes us eat. It is the totality of our experience (culture, advertising, sugar, fat, and our own biology) that makes us eat. To change how we do something, we first have to recognize what we are doing and why.

Alongside all the sensations that we experience when we eat, there are two drivers of how much we eat. These two dynamic forces are feeling full (satiety) and feeling hungry.

How Much Did I Really Have to Eat to Be Full? I thought about the reasons I ate and how I ate. When I wanted to lose weight, I would count carbs, count calories, increase my activity, drink water, and do all the things I knew would make me feel satisfied. I also recognized that there had to be something else that I should be doing. I soon realized that I did not know what "full" actually meant. How much did I have to eat to be full?

For years I had repeated the mantra that if 1 is starving and 10 is that overstuffed and bloated feeling that comes from eating too much, then the goal was to be at 5. The Japanese have a common expression *hara hachi bu,* which means to fill your stomach (*hara*) to 80 percent. It usually takes a while for our brain to register that we are full, so by stopping at 80 percent, we often find a little later that satiety has been reached.

25

Satiety Is the Goal. As I thought about what it means to be full, I realized that perhaps I did not really know what that meant. I started to consider what a full stomach is and how large a full stomach gets. I remember hearing some people comment that their stomachs had been stretched because they were accustomed to eating so much food. I thought about the images of people competing in food eating contests.

Have you ever seen the videos of the food contests where people stuff more hot dogs down their throats than most of us could eat in a week? I did not know how that was possible, especially as most of the huge eaters were not huge in size.

Human biology is such that the size of your stomach is not related to your weight or waist size. It is a surprise to many that most people have stomachs that are about the same size. Your stomach usually can hold up to 1½ quarts of food or liquid, but it can expand and contract. It can hold as little as one ounce or as much as a gallon of liquid, at which point it is near the point of rupture.

While your stomach is pretty modest in size, your intestines are very, very long. The small intestine is about one inch in diameter and 20 feet long and can hold 188 cubic inches, or 3.2 quarts. Your large intestine is about 3 inches in diameter and 5 feet long and can hold 424 cubic inches, or 7.3 quarts. That means that you can hold a lot more food than you really need.

This information left me with a lot of questions. What does being full really mean? How full is full? Why do some people not know when they are full? Maybe some underlying condition makes it hard for some people to tell when they are full.

Or maybe the reason it was hard to know what "full" meant was that some people were addicted to food: in other words, food had become their drug. According to the National Institute on Drug Abuse, drug addiction is "a chronic, relapsing brain disease that is characterized by compulsive drug seeking and use, despite harmful consequences. It is considered a brain disease because drugs change the brain; they change its structure and how it works. These brain changes can be long-lasting and can lead to many harmful, often self-destructive, behaviors."[1] Those words did not seem to apply either to me or to the people I know who were trying to manage their eating.

As I thought about it more, I realized that the reason that the addiction model did not work is that most research on addiction focuses on substances (drugs and alcohol) or behaviors (gambling and sex) that are not biologically essential to life. You cannot just give up eating, because you have to eat in order to stay alive. That makes most addictions very different from how many of us feel about food or eating.

For example, at the most basic level, one possible approach to treating most addictions is simply to abstain, or "go cold turkey." That approach would not work when it comes to eating. It would be unreasonable— not to mention dangerous and irresponsible — to tell people that in order to manage their weight they just had to give up food. That is why the research that focused on eating as analogous to drug addiction did not strike me as relevant. The addiction model was not helpful in understanding the reasons why people have trouble managing their weight. The need for food is rooted in a biological imperative.

As I gathered more research, I reviewed what is known about binge eating. While there is much in the popular press about this eating disorder, I realized that most people who want to improve their health by losing weight were not engaging in what is clinically described as binge eating. Even though binge eating is the most common eating disorder in the U.S., the absolute number of people who engage in this type of behavior is actually low. What we know is that binge eating is more common in women than men and, interestingly, women are affected as young adults while men are affected in middle age. A person with a binge eating disorder:

- eats large amounts of food in a short period, for example, every two hours.
- is not able to control overeating, so, for example, is unable to stop eating or control the amount of food.
- eats food very fast each time.
- keeps eating even when full (gorging) or until uncomfortably full.
- eats even though not hungry.
- eats alone (in secret).
- feels guilty, disgusted, ashamed, or depressed after eating so much.

Even though the exact cause of binge eating is still unknown, what we do know is that there are many factors that could cause it. Possible causes include some characteristic inherited from a close relative who also has trouble managing weight, changes in the chemicals in your brain, negative emotions (being upset or stressed), depression, or even unhealthy dieting, such as not eating enough nutritious food or skipping meals. Someone who is truly a binge eater should seek help and support from a mental health professional.

Of course, there are also some very rare genetic conditions that cause people to eat to excess regardless of how full they may actually be.

Those people have a problem with a chromosome 15 segment (Prader-Willi Syndrome) ever since they were conceived. This genetic problem causes them to gain weight.

Research has shown that some people with excess weight do not have the same ability to know when they are full (satiety) as people of normal weight.[2] Perhaps knowing that you are full is lot harder than we thought. Knowing how much your body needs is very important for your health, but knowing when you are full is just as essential. The answer seemed to lie in knowing when you are hungry and recognizing that there are different degrees of hunger. This awareness is your key to being able to eat a healthy amount of food at the right time.

About Being Hungry

I was paying for my purchases at a major department store when I started to flip through the pages of the fashion magazine that happened to be by the register. As I looked at the faces of the models I commented to my friend, "I do not know why models have those expressions on their faces. They look unhappy and sometimes even surly." Without skipping a beat or even looking up from the register, the well-coifed saleswoman said, "They look that way because they are hungry."

As I looked at the next picture, I imagined a balloon caption above the model's head saying, "I am so hungry." The more I flipped the pages and looked at the different ads, the more I realized that most of the models have an expression that says, "I'm hungry" or "I haven't eaten for days." And on those rare pages where the image included a happier face the caption could have read, "At last... I see some food in the distance" or "Yes! A cheeseburger!"

I know that we live in a society that glorifies being thin. Too thin. The distorted body images that are celebrated are just as damaging as the belief that a woman can never be too thin. I actually felt bad for the many models who have to be underweight to keep their jobs. More recently, the death of some high-profile models have even led a few countries to outlaw the use of models who are underweight.

Yet the images that are everywhere are predominantly of people who look very hungry even though they are dressed in expensive clothes and wear too much makeup. If the same models wore tattered clothes, the images would suggest malnourishment. It did not make sense that we simultaneously glorify thinness and vilify being hungry.

For most of us, being hungry is bad—it is a state to be avoided. If you feel hungry, you eat, because you want to avoid getting even hungrier. Even worse, being unable to satisfy your hunger seems to imply that you do not have the means to provide for yourself. If you are hungry, you must have failed in some way. Nevertheless, I was beginning to think there might be a role for hunger in healthy eating. We all know that feeling hungry is a basic need that tends to override all other senses and even rationality. When someone is truly hungry, the need to satisfy that need tends to prevail over everything else. The key is learning to distinguish between true hunger and hunger stemming from poor eating habits.

The French concept of hunger is different than the American concept . . . We value hunger as a way to more fully appreciate what we eat. Dr. France Bellisle, 2007.[3]

I remember distinctly hearing Dr. Bellisle utter those words. We were at a meeting talking about healthy eating, and I thought that she was so right. It would be against all our beliefs to say that hunger was acceptable. How could anyone value hunger? The idea that in order to eat in a healthy way you had to be hungry was perplexing and provocative. I wondered whether her statement contained some truth that could be useful to the many people who try to manage their weight.

Perhaps the reason that French people were thinner had to do more with how they approached their food. Did French people really accept hunger as a comfortable state?

In my personal experience and in that of the many women and men who spoke to me as they struggled with their weight, being hungry did not lead to an increased appreciation of food. It just made us want to eat more. Being hungry meant that we needed to get food right away. Even worse, people found that they became ravenous and were more likely to eat everything that was in front of them. Hunger seemed a trigger for mindless eating. A buffet was less a selection of different foods than an opportunity to feed at a trough. Nevertheless, Dr. Bellisle's comment echoed in my head. Part of me felt that there was a truth hidden in her words.

While we eat, obviously, for nutrition, our behaviors and thoughts about when to eat and what to eat are based on many other factors. We all know that hunger is seen as a drive and motivator. Hunters and gatherers were not engaged in their respective activities for pleasure but for survival. As we consider the reasons why we eat, we find that there are many. Some of us may eat only for nourishment, while others experience hedonic hunger; that is, the drive to eat foods even when no replenishment of energy is needed. There are many reasons why we eat, and I learned from talking to others that hunger has many meanings.

My understanding of different languages made me particularly sensitive to the notion that words have deeper, cultural, meanings. The meaning of a word has a depth that is a combination of the literal translation provided by a computer, the intent of the speaker, and the art of expressing nuance. While a picture may be worth a thousand words, the carefully selected word can generate a thousand images. Hunger is one of those special words. What it means is rooted in culture.

In their research, scholars P. J. Rogers and C. A. Hardman define hunger as the absence of fullness.[4] Certainly, the meaning of "hunger" in English and more specifically for people in the United States is negative. That is why some philanthropic organizations successfully raise money by showing pictures of people who look hungry and are malnourished. We do not want anyone to be hungry, and the key message is that hunger is a state to be avoided. Being hungry implies that you are not being taken care of and are unable to provide for your basic needs. This is even more so among immigrants or the children of immigrants. Surely Dr. Bellisle did not mean to say that in France it was okay to be starving.

To better understand her earlier comment, I went back to Dr. Bellisle and asked her about her comment years before regarding hunger. She said that I had remembered her comment exactly and expanded on it, adding, "of course it is about mild hunger, the kind of hunger that people are likely to experience between their daily meals. It is nice to feel hungry at the start of a meal."

It was a linguistic and cultural nuance. Giving the concept of hunger a more positive connotation was essential. The new meaning was closer to desirous than to starving. Mild hunger was not something that I even knew how to register. As it is for most people, hunger for me was a light that was either on or off. When it was on, it was time to eat. I had to recalibrate, to learn to recognize degrees of hunger ranging from acceptable to unacceptable. And I had to learn to embrace being a little hungry.

Rethinking was essential, and with that, the practice of embracing mild hunger began.

For years I had advocated modifying how much we eat by using a 10- point scale where 1 was starving and 10 was stuffed. The goal was to know when you reached 5. This is still important. But now there was the added dimension that I had been searching for. In order to manage my weight, I would teach myself that it was okay to be a little hungry. It was okay to be at 4. I had to relearn that when I desired food, I did not have to satisfy that hunger immediately, nor did I have to stuff myself when I did eat. I could wait until my next meal and eat a reasonable amount of food.

It took a lot of work to learn what was the acceptable level of mild hunger for me and for my body. I did not want to give myself a hunger headache, nor did I want to delay eating until I felt faint. I had to relearn when to eat. I already knew how much to eat and the importance of exercise, but now I had to teach myself to be hungry. Of course, when friends asked me how I lost weight, I responded that one of my new practices was that I learned to be hungry. The typical response was one of disbelief, or that there had to be another way. But really, there is no other way. The reason most people boomerang is that they go back to eating as they did before. They may learn new skills about what to eat, but they never learn to enjoy mild hunger.

I have learned that if I do not eat immediately when I feel hungry and I just wait a bit, I tend not to eat as much. It is as if waiting a little bit decreased how "hungry" I felt. Not responding to that initial "I'm hungry" feeling is really helpful for me. Alice

People may learn new eating patterns and increase their activity, but the boomerang effect—gaining back all the weight that was lost—is inevitable unless they make a huge change in their practices about when to eat and how much to eat. Learning to be hungry was the huge change in my thinking and my behavior.

Allowing myself to be a little hungry was different. Initially it was tough, but being okay with mild hunger changed everything.

What did being hungry mean? Well, I wasn't sure what it would mean, since I was accustomed to eating whenever I was hungry. And I was hungry a lot of the time but rarely stayed hungry for long. Hunger was a feeling that I had to learn to calibrate so that I could live with it. It became clear that hunger was not an all-or-nothing feeling, but actually had a range. The challenge was to learn what was okay, or mild hunger.

Dr. Bellisle clarified what acceptable hunger is. "[It is] moderate in intensity but [is] also short in duration. It occurs a few minutes or even an hour before a meal (or another eating occasion) when it is wonderful to have [an] appetite. The idea is not about enduring pain or distress; it is to be sensitive to your bodily sensations that signal the normal fluctuations of appetite. If you want to experience satiety (and enjoy it), then it is normal to also experience hunger (and hopefully be able to enjoy a moderate and short-lived sensation of 'wanting' as the recent scientific literature puts it)."[5]

She went further and spoke of her own experience, "Personally, I do enjoy the moderate feeling of hunger I am experiencing right now, as I am writing this letter to you at 11:22 in the morning. I had breakfast by 7, I will have a satisfactory and palatable lunch in about one hour, and frankly I am very pleased to feel the need for food. If you just look at the sensation, it is not unpleasant at all. The adequate response here is not: rush to your fridge, but rather: just sit back and enjoy it."

It was interesting how friends and colleagues responded to me during the first few months, when I was trying this new approach to eating. When people asked, "How are you?" I would respond with a heartfelt "I am hungry." I was surprised at the response that I got, as it was not the answer they expected. Many seemed uncomfortable with it. Most people were perplexed, and some offered to get me something to eat. Friends and colleagues had a hard time understanding that I really was hungry and that it was okay. They did not know how to respond.

Some of the responses were thought-provoking. There were many suggestions about what to eat to reduce my hunger, ranging from kale juice to fruit. Another common response was, "It will take a few weeks and then you won't be hungry anymore." To that I usually responded, "No, I have been hungry for months and it is okay. It will be this way for the rest of my life. I appreciate being a little hungry, and when I do eat now, I appreciate it even more."

That was a big new insight to managing my weight. I had to learn that it was okay to be a little hungry.

I had always counted calories and carbs and followed all sorts of weight loss plans. I had increased exercise and made sure that I was healthy, but I had not managed to lose weight and keep it off.

This time, what made all the difference was learning that a little hunger is part of the enjoyment of eating and an essential practice for maintaining a healthy weight. This would have to remain a life-long part of how I approached food. To make it easier for myself, I came up with things to do when I was a little hungry and things I needed to avoid.

What to Do When You Are a Little Hungry

Learning to be a little hungry takes practice. You have to get used to it. Being a little hungry should be a cue for you to do something else that is constructive. It is key to do something you *like* to do instead of satisfying your mild hunger. Rather than eating when you have some healthy hunger, you need to get *busy* doing something that is not related to food. Find what activity works best for you. Some things you may want to consider include:

1. Communicate with others.
2. Send a text message.
3. Check items on the Internet.
4. Do some window/screen shopping.
5. Use my MyFitnessPal and plan your next meal.
6. Read a book.
7. Drink a glass of water, coffee, or tea.
8. Sort through your inbox.
9. Go for a walk.
10. Walk your pet.
11. Chat with family, friends, or colleagues.
12. Do your laundry.
13. Clean or organize a closet, desk, or drawer.
14. Call someone you have not spoken to for a while.
15. Begin to prepare a dish that takes a long time to make.
16. Write a long letter or an email to a friend.
17. Watch a movie.
18. Go for a drive.

19. Offer to help someone with a task.
20. Finish a project.

Places to Avoid When You Are Hungry

- the kitchen
- areas where there is good food
- areas where you can smell food
- places that give out food to sample
- the supermarket

---

[1] National Institute on Drug Abuse. Accessed April 17, 2015 http://www.drugabuse.gov/publications/media-guide/science-drug-abuse-addiction-basics

[2] Herbert, B.M. and Pollatos, O. "Attenuated Interoceptive Sensitivity in Overweight and Obese Individuals," *Eating Behaviors* Vol 15(3), August, 2014, Pgs. 445-448. DOI: http://dx.doi.org/10.1016/j.eatbeh.2014.06.002

[3] Bellisle, France. Personal e-mail communication. March 17, 2015

[4] Rogers, P.J., and Hardman, C.A. "Food Reward. "What It Is and How to Measure It." *Appetite*, Vol 90, Jul 1, 2015, Pgs. 136-143 DOI: http://dx.doi.org/10.1016/j.appet.2015.02.032

[5] Bellisle, France. Personal e-mail communication. February 8, 2016.

CHAPTER 3
Tame The External Forces That Make You Eat

As a psychologist and a person who began by wanting to lose a modest 10 pounds, I knew that if I wanted to be successful, I would have to apply the behavioral theories that I know are so effective in other areas to help me manage my weight. Unfortunately, **the evidence was clear that while many weight loss programs show promise, it was uncertain what would actually be effective for each person**.[1]

I knew this from all the studies, but also because I am the typical person who would follow a plan for a while and eventually stop. Weight loss programs may be elegant and intellectually seductive, but they seemed to have failed me as well as many others. I wanted to find an answer. This was not about a theory about weight loss or a particular weight loss program; this was about my life.

As I tried to tease out the intellectual exercises from the practical application, I was always humbled by the knowledge that changing personal behavior is very hard to do even when someone wants to change. Decades as a clinician have made me appreciate the hard work my patients do outside of our one-hour sessions. My patients want to change some aspect of their lives, but even with all the personal motivation, it is very difficult. Teaching them about the triggers that push them in the wrong direction is as essential as teaching them new skills is. Just as important, if not more so, is working with them to give them a new mental approach or framework for applying the new skills.

It was as I struggled with the idea of how I was going to lose those initial pounds that I realized that when it comes to maintaining a healthy weight, establishing a new way of approaching food would be essential. My challenge was to investigate all the drivers to overeating that exist, and then decipher what are the factors that maintain this undesired behavior.

While there were many barriers, I knew that a lack of knowledge about what to eat and what to do was not the problem. Like most people who have had to manage their weight, I could distinguish healthy foods from unhealthy foods, and I knew the caloric count of most of what ate. This is true for many of us who have tried to maintain a healthy weight. Most people seemed to know what to eat and how much they should eat.

Similarly, people were aware that it was important to exercise. People had the knowledge to say what they wanted to do, but they were unable to actually do it.

Decades of behavioral research demonstrates that knowledge alone is not enough to change our eating behavior. Even having insight by itself does not lead us to change what we do. There are many aspects of our daily lives that make it difficult for us to apply the facts that we know. Most important of all, there are key aspects of the world in which we live that play unique and critical roles in our ability to use our knowledge to manage what and when we eat. Our culture and the role of advertising are two external forces that drive us to eat even when we are not hungry.

Culture

Culture is something we think about when we look at others. We study the sexual behaviors of people who live in other places, examine the cuisine of people who consider food preparation a family activity, and all too often we draw conclusions that are more judgmental than relevant. Still, each of us is part of a culture or many cultures, and understanding the impact of culture on our decisions is essential.

Everything we think, say, or do is wrapped up in culture and the cultural context in which we find ourselves. Culture has nurtured some of us, while for others it has been a source of major conflict and upheaval. Regardless, what we do does not occur in a vacuum. The interactions we have with each other help define much of what constructs our daily life.

In particular, culture drives and defines our relationship with food. Living in a particular culture is expressed through when we eat, what we eat, how much we eat and even the meaning certain foods. The connections, while sometimes subtle, are powerful drivers of our own eating behavior.

For example, most celebrations involve eating as part of the communal experience. Not having a piece of cake at a birthday party may be considered rude. If you go to a wedding and pass on the cake, you are not truly celebrating the new couple. If you do not join in the champagne toast at a celebration, you are not really celebrating the event. And if you are a guest and do not eat some of everything that was specially prepared for the meal, the host may be hurt or insulted. Partaking of food with others is part of what we all do even when we may not want to.

We often find ourselves in situations where it is easy to eat without noticing that we're not hungry or how much we are eating. These cultural pushes are characteristics that push us to do something and they are inherent within a given situation because of the cultural messages of what you are expected to do. If the custom when eating out with others is for each person to have an appetizer, main course, and dessert, then it is natural to feel compelled to order the same amount of food whether you are hungry or not. People often feel that they would be viewed as odd if they ordered an extra appetizer instead of the main course even when that is all they can or should eat.

Our environment not only sets the stage but also constrains and induces us by defining what is acceptable. And in our culture, eating is social. It is very clear that what is acceptable in our culture, where we live, and to those with whom we interact are powerful drivers of how and what we eat.

In 1999, Boyd Swinburne and his colleagues, leading researchers on excess weight, were writing about looking at all the factors that make it easy for individuals to gain weight.[2] Their model looked at specific factors: "Physical (what is available), economic (what are the costs), political (what are the 'rules'), and sociocultural (what are the attitudes and beliefs)." The purpose of their research was to identify the strength of each factor as well as the interactions between and among each one. The implication was that once you understood the factors, you would be able to develop a plan of action to reduce whatever was driving people to eat in ways that were not healthy.

It turns out that *all* the factors in Swinburne and Egger's model (what is available, the costs, the attitudes and beliefs about food and eating) play key roles in our daily life in very intricate ways. What we choose to eat is based on the availability and affordability of food. The choices we make are further modified by our need to eat quickly so we can get back to whatever we were doing. The interplay of these factors is intricate, dynamic, and subject to changing pressures. This is especially so because most of us spend a considerable part of our day away from home. As a result, our choices are limited to what is fast to eat and easy on our wallet.

Take for instance what happens if when and how we eat is defined by the need to eat fast or in a hurried fashion. We inhale our food and miss important cues from our bodies. It takes time for the stomach to register that it is full. It takes even longer for the brain to recognize that we are no longer hungry. Since we tend to be rushed when we eat, we end up eating more than we need to because we eat so fast that we do not have the time to receive the signal from our stomach to our brain that we are full. All this makes controlling how much we eat difficult.

As excess weight became a challenge for more and more people, additional research naturally followed. In 2011, the highly respected medical journal *Lancet* published several articles synthesizing what was known about excess weight and its management. Several authors thought about the findings of all the articles and, after a thorough analysis, concluded that the only thing that was clear was the need to better understand what worked.[3] While there were many methods intended to help people manage their weight, the basic information on weight and the outcomes for the different methods were not moving the dial on the scale in the desired direction. The authors called for more study of what actually happens under the different weight reduction programs that are available. Most alarming to some, but so very comforting to me, was the message to the field that *"assumptions about speed and sustainability of weight loss are wrong."*[4]

Nevertheless, we have developed a variety of explanations about what makes us eat and how food affects us. The not-so-good news is that the debate about exactly what is going on that makes people gain weight is ongoing.

Four years later, in 2015, *Lancet* published another series of papers that called for a rethinking of weight management.[5] In their review, the authors concluded that it was critical to understand that eating is the result of the "reciprocal nature of the interaction between the environment and the individual,"[6] where the information we get from everything around us reinforces unhealthy food choices and behaviors.[7] The authors went on to say, "Today's food environments exploit people's biological, psychological, social, and economic vulnerabilities, making it easier for them to eat unhealthy foods. This reinforces preferences and demands for foods of poor nutritional quality, furthering the unhealthy food environments."[8]

In short, it was hard for a person to eat healthy because the cues and drivers around them were pushing them towards unhealthy choices and to be hungry.

In other words, our culture also makes it very hard to eat healthy foods or in healthy amounts. Consider the message behind the statement in the familiar ad, "You can't eat just one." Visualize yourself eating chips. Do you ever think of a plate of chips? No, it is always a bowl, and a bowl holds a lot more.

Corinna Hawkes and her co-investigators[9] went even further when they stated, "Effective food-policy actions are tailored to the preference, behavioral, socioeconomic, and demographic characteristics of the people they seek to support, are designed to work through the mechanisms through which they have greatest effect, and are implemented as part of a combination of mutually reinforcing actions."

What that means is that the environment around us, the way foods are manufactured and processed, and the marketing of specific foods are all aimed at encouraging us to eat more than necessary or choose unhealthy food.

For some, this may seem like more of an economic issue. Some people are "forced" to purchase foods that they would rather not eat or foods that they know are not as healthy because they have a limited amount to spend on food. This is more likely to happen when a person is buying food not just for themselves but for a family. Too often, a person is given basically two choices: buy the less healthy food and have something to put on the table or try to find a healthier and equally reasonable alternative. Fortunately, food manufacturers are increasingly making foods that are healthier and less expensive. To eat healthy and on a budget there are some steps you can take:

- 🐾 Eat fruits and vegetables that are in season.
- 🐾 Celebrate eating less that is healthier instead of eating larger amounts of unhealthy foods.
- 🐾 Drink water instead of sugar-sweetened beverages.
- 🐾 Make a grocery list from items that are on sale.

With so many types of powerful drivers, it should not be surprising that eating healthy is a challenge. People are inundated by environmental cues, flavors, and advertising, all of which drive them to eat regardless of their level of hunger or nutritional needs. This creates circumstances that drive us to eat even when we are not hungry—an environment that researchers call "obesogenic."

Living in an obesogenic culture means that social cues and cultural norms that encourage unhealthy eating are everywhere. They pervade our daily life. Recently I arrived at an airport and needed to rush to eat because the security lines were much longer than expected. When I went to the food court, I found that my options were the familiar ones that dominate most public venues. Unfortunately, there were few choices that would be healthy and satisfying. Whether you are at a bus stop, train station, mall, airport, your own neighborhood, or your car, the foods that are easily available, affordable, and consumable are often the ones that push us to the wrong side of the scale.

Sadly, the research on culture and creating an environment that promotes healthy eating, also called a leptogenic environment, has been minimal. Most of what has been studied focuses on the effects of the physical or architectural environment on activity. That is why we now know the positive effects of having places where adults can safely walk or exercise close to where they live. While these studies have helped encourage more safe places to walk and options for exercise, they have done little to change our environment with respect to how culture drives how and when we eat.

When it comes to eating, our culture encourages us to eat more than we need to eat: it is obesogenic. There is very little that promotes healthy eating. Perhaps a better way to understand the culture would be to consider what influences the specific choices people make. The many factors that drive people to eat need to be examined at deeper levels. When we think of how we make food choices, a major area that needs to be considered is the role of advertising in our culture.

Advertising

Many of us like to believe that after decades of exposure, we have all been inoculated against the impact of advertising. It is natural to be a bit skeptical that advertising still has a major impact on our choices. But of course it does. If it did not change behavior, no company would spend money on advertising.

Most of the studies on advertising and unhealthy food choices focus on research on children. The 2011 *Time* article by Alice Park called "It's the Ads, Stupid:

Why TV Leads to Obesity"[10] was quite disturbing. The title summarized her findings that "the average American child sees nearly 8,000 commercials on TV for food and beverages, and only 165 of these are for nutritious options like fruits and vegetables." Advertising to children is very successful. To some people, it may seem illogical to advertise to children, since they are not the ones who make the family budget or buy the groceries. But advertising to children sells billions of dollars of products.

The success of this marketing strategy involves a classic two-part process. Marketers have learned, first, that children can be swayed to want a product regardless of its value, and, second, that once the children are convinced to want a product, children can get their parents to buy the product. Fundamentally, advertising to children depends on the ability to induce children to want to eat a particular food or drink. There is no attempt to inform them about health or nutrition.

Most important of all at a time when all efforts should focus on developing skills to make good food choices, children are shown images that encourage the exact opposite. Take a close look at the items that are listed in the typical children's menu, and it's easy to understand how the unhealthy choices get started early and are promoted.

At the same time, there is a lack of research on the effects of advertising on adults. Perhaps that is because there is a belief that adults know how to be selective and what they choose they do from their own free will. We should know better. Food ads are designed to make people believe that certain foods or beverages will make them more popular, stronger, better, more athletic, sexier, or more like the person who is promoting the product.

Whether we want to admit it or not, the impact of advertising on adults is huge. Companies advertise and market their products because it is a successful strategy to get us to buy their product. There are cues all around us that are geared to getting us to buy and eat products that may not represent the best choices.

With people watching less television and reading fewer magazines, the nature of advertising has had to change to capture today's consumer. The day of the single campaign that reaches everybody is gone, and people are reached on a very personal level with individualized messages that match their digital profile in multiple ways. The companies that sell us products have learned and adapted to the new ways people want to be reached.

The messages are increasingly tailored to the individual, while the few health messages tend to get lost. And sometimes a health claim that is emphasized by the producer of a food or beverage distracts the consumer from the unhealthy side of their product. Yogurt is a good example. It is often marketed as healthy and natural. That may be true for some products, but when you read the label, you may be surprised to find the amount of sugar some manufacturers add.

We are also learning that the consequences of advertising go beyond just getting you to buy a specific product. It also gets adults to eat more in general. In one experiment adults watched programs that either had commercials that promoted snacking, promoted the benefits of good nutrition, or had no food advertising. The findings were dramatic: "Adults consumed more of both healthy and unhealthy snack foods following exposure to snack food advertising compared to the other conditions."[11]

The research showed that the impact of the advertising went beyond the specific product—it actually made people eat more.

Most people know that advertising is about getting you to do something or buy something. It is not about empowering you to make the best choices based on complete information. Rather, advertising is about giving you the information that will get you to buy the product that is being sold.

The false messages in many of the ads we see are embedded within false images. Just think of the last ad you saw. The people are thinner than most of us, even though they may be indulging in products that would make anyone gain weight. When we view ads, we somehow forget what we know and accept the suggestion that you can eat in an unhealthy way and still be thin. We need to look at food ads more critically and recognize that they are there to make us desire the product and believe that the product is a good choice. There are very few ads that tell you to eat less or eat healthy. Everything around us is geared to getting us to eat more.

To make matters worse too often there is misleading or even deceptive advertising about weight loss products, plans, or procedures. The images in the ads tend to be of people who lost a lot more weight than most of us need to lose or where it visually made a tremendous difference. We forget that too often the images have either been altered or taken at special angles. In many cases the images are accompanied by a testimonial or junk science. Sometimes the spokesperson is someone we respect or want to emulate. But if any of these products or plans were truly successful, it would shut down all the others. The genius of the weight loss industry lies in getting us to buy products that at most have temporary benefits. Eating healthy is a lifelong activity; it is not something we do only once and then stop.

That is why the work to develop new practices is essential. It is by changing what we do now and in the future that we can achieve and maintain a healthy approach to eating.

Each of us needs to understand what pushes us to eat.

As I thought about my own situation, I started to discover new data that could better explain the challenges that I and countless others were encountering. As I dug into some of the recent research, I found a more complicated explanation of what makes us eat what we eat and what makes us eat more than we should, going beyond the urgings of our obesogenic culture.

I knew it was hard to lose weight and even harder to maintain the weight loss. I had lived that experience throughout my life. So had most of the people who would openly talk to me about their attempts to manage their weight. While most of the research highlighted one conceptual model or some weight loss program, I was disappointed that most of the studies that I read looked at just one or two things to do to lose weight.

We know that each person is pushed to eat by a unique set of both subtle and obvious drivers.

Each researcher seems to have a favorite explanation for the worldwide increase in the number of people with excess weight. Explanations include too many calories, lack of physical activity, too much junk food being eaten, too much junk food being advertised, too many chemicals in the environment that throw the endocrine system out of balance, gluttony, unhealthy beverages, genes, stress, bad choices of individuals, low income, food deserts, and many others. The list is very, very long. The problem I saw with the published research was that it missed what was happening at the individual level.

Talking to people made it clear that some, all, or, most likely, a combination of those factors played a role in how well individuals could manage their weight. Additionally, even for a single individual, the factors that determined what he or she ate could shift in a day, a week, or a month. It seemed pointless to do research that only looked at one or two factors as the determinants of what people would eat, since there were always more factors involved.

At the same time, the typical research model handles individual differences by statistically cancelling them out. That means it is not designed to capture, and is likely to ignore, the interaction among factors at the individual level. Even worse, what is often omitted are the intervening or unexpected occurrences that are part of a person's life and may limit one's ability to manage weight.

How true. For me, if the stress is because I am not sure how to handle a situation, I become very hungry, as if by eating I will come up with a solution. If the stress is because I am deeply hurt or upset, I cannot eat. It is as if my body does not even want to work at digesting until I can resolve or at least reason out why I feel so hurt. Alice

Hearing the stories of those who were attempting to lose weight and trying to keep it off confirmed that a different array of factors has a role in each person's eating behavior. The differences among the people I spoke to were huge. Additionally, for each person there was variability in the combination of factors that influenced what and when he or she ate on a daily basis. One day a person would be so stressed and upset that that eating was impossible, while in another situation stress made the same person ravenous. Consequently, the conclusions from research on stress and the ability of people to control what they eat is not surprising. By looking at changes in a person's brain, Silvia Maier, a researcher at the Laboratory for Social and Neural Systems Research at the University of Zurich, and her colleagues documented that stress reduced self-control.[12]

Obviously, there is also variability from person to person as to what makes them eat and what makes them stop eating. The factors that frame whether or not a person is successful in managing their weight are not static. They change at different points in our lives.

So, applying all this research to myself, I realized that the solution was elsewhere and that I had to apply the cognitive behavioral principles that I had been taught to support a new approach that would help people to eat in a way that is helpful.

The challenge in changing how we eat is to recalibrate what we think about food and our relationship with what we eat. It's not just about going on a diet, following a plan, or eating special foods. While we may have good information about how to eat in a way to manage our weight, our attempts to do so are overwhelmed by the pull of the cultural messages about food and the advertising that are all around us. As a result of these factors, our senses and good intentions are drowned out by cultural messages that are amplified through advertising.

---

[1]   Baranowski, T., Cullen, K.W., Nicklas, T., Thompson, D., and, Baranowski, J. "Are Current Health Behavioral Change Models Helpful in Guiding Prevention of Weight Gain Efforts?" *Obesity Research. Special Issue: Obesity, Lifestyle, and Weight Management.* Vol. 11, Issue S10, Pgs. 23S–43S, October, 2003. DOI: http://dx.doi.org/10.1038/oby.2003.222.

[2]   Swinburn, B., Egger, G., and, Raza, F. "Dissecting Obesogenic Environments: The Development and Application of a Framework for Identifying and Prioritizing Environmental Interventions for Obesity," *Preventive Medicine.* Volume 29, Issue 6, December 1999, Pgs. 563–570

[3]   "Urgently needed: a framework convention for obesity control," *The Lancet.* August 27, 2011; 378: 741. DOI: http://dx.doi.org/10.1016/S0140-6736(11) 61356-1

[4]   Ibid.

[5]   Kleinert, S. and Horton, R. "Rethinking and Reframing Obesity," *The Lancet*, London EC2Y 5AS, UK 2. Accessed April 17, 2015. www.thelancet.com Published online February 18, 2015 DOI: http://dx.doi.org/10.1016/S0140-6736(15)60163-5

[6]   Roberto, C.A.; Swinburn, B.A.; Huang, T.T-K.; Costa, S.; Ashe, M.; Zwicker, L.; Cawlet, J.H. and Brownell, K.D. "Patchy Progress on Obesity Prevention: Emerging Examples, Entrenched Barriers, and New Thinking," *The Lancet* 2015. Published Online Feb 18,2015. DOI: http://dx.doi.org/10.1016/S0140- 6736(14)61744-X

[7]   Kleinert, S. and Horton, R. "Comment: Rethinking and Reframing Obesity." *Lancet 2015*; Published online February 18, 2015. DOI: http://dx.doi.org/10.1016/ S0140-6736(15)60163-5

[8]   "Obesity 2015. Executive Summary," *The Lancet*; Published online February 18, 2015.

[9]   Hawkes, C.; Smith, T.G.; Jewell, J.; Wardle, J.; Hammond, R.; Friel, S.; Thow, A.M. and Kain, J. "Smart Food Policies for Obesity Prevention." *The Lancet*. Published online February 18, 2015 DOI: http://dx.doi.org/10.1016/S0140- 6736(14)61745-1 Accessed April 17, 2015.

[10] Park, A. "It's the Ads, Stupid: Why TV Leads to Obesity," *Time*, June 27, 2011.

[11] Harris, J. L., Bargh, J.A., and Brownell, K.D. "Priming Effects of Television Food Advertising on Eating Behavior," *Health Psychology*, Vol 28(4), July, 2009, Pgs. 404-413. DOI: http://dx.doi.org/10.1037/a0014399

[12] Maier, S.U.; Makwana, A.B. and Hare, T.A. "Acute Stress Impairs Self-Control in Goal-Directed Choice by Altering Multiple Functional Connections within the Brain's Decision Circuits." *Neuron*, Vol. 87, Issue 3, Pgs. 521-631, Aug. 5, 2015. DOI: http://dx.doi.org/10.1016/j.neuron.2015.07.005

CHAPTER 4
The Impact of Your Biology, Sugar, and Fat

The previous chapter explained some of the external forces that drive you to eat, but in order to make your journey successful, you need to understand the internal forces that can undermine your journey so that you can work around them. Each person brings a unique set of experiences to their relationship with food, and on top of that, their own biology tempers how they will progress on any plan.

Your Biology

In November 2015 Dr. David Zeevi and his colleagues shared the findings of their study, which looked at the glucose levels of 800 volunteers every week and their response to 46,898 meals.[1] They collected health and lifestyle on the volunteers. Each person was also connected to a device that monitored blood sugar level every five minutes for an entire week. Their key finding was that even when people ate the same foods, their bodies did not respond in the same way. For some people, eating sushi increased their blood sugar level more than eating ice cream. In fact, what they found was great variability. Their conclusion was that having the same dietary guidelines for everyone may not be as useful as was assumed.

Part of the explanation for their finding was knowledge about the microbiome, which is the assortment of microbes that reside in our stomach. Scientists now know that some of these microbes have a major impact on how our body uses sugar and how much insulin is released. The microbes play an intricate role in how much we eat and how what we eat gets metabolized. We know that there are microbes in the gut that activate hormones that tell the brain what to do with what you are consuming and even whether or not you are full.

This is a growing area of research. We now know that there are good microbes and bad microbes. The intricacies of how these microbes work are slowly being uncovered. When the microbes in our gut are not working well, they can distort how the energy in our fat cells is used.[2]

That your genes play a role in your size is expected. There is evidence suggesting that "as much as 21 percent of BMI variation can be accounted for by common genetic variation."[3] This means that genes have a role in your BMI: one more reason that what works for one person may not work for someone else. New pathways and relationships between genes and excess weight are being found every day.[4] Each one of us has to find our own path to manage our weight regardless of what we may have inherited. For some of us, that means that what we inherited may provide an impediment to managing our weight and our challenge is to figure out how best to work around it.

The translation of these findings and information about genes into specifics that actually help people will take decades. Meanwhile, we know for sure that the best eating plan must be tailored and personalized for you.

In developing a plan, we need to know the relationship between certain foods and our desire to eat. There are companies that use this science to make us buy and eat more, as some foods have a larger effect on us than the calories consumed. It is with this in mind that I present some key facts on sugar and fat and the interplay with how our body uses these nutrients that can undermine our efforts to eat in a healthy way.

Sugar

When I started to develop my new way of approaching food, I knew that I had to be honest about what I would or would not give up. Early on, I also recognized that there were items that I enjoyed immensely. Coffee with sugar-in-the-raw is essential to my well-being. I look forward to my morning coffee (about two twelve-ounce cups) and the two teaspoons of unrefined sugar that get gently stirred into each cup. Although I am not a person who craves desserts, I do like to have some sweets, particularly in my morning coffee. I accepted that regardless of what I changed, some items I would not remove from my daily routine. I still have my sugar in my morning coffee.

While we all know that sweet is nice, too much is not good for us. Sweetness comes in many products that we enjoy, including table sugar, agave, honey, and other products. And to add to the list of sweeteners, you have to remember that carbs (or carbohydrates) are broken down by the body into sugar.

Keep in mind that sugar (glucose) is essential. To be healthy we all need some sugar. Glucose is the source of energy for many of the functions of our cells. Even our brain needs some glucose to work properly. But how much sugar is enough?

When it comes to sugar, the story is complicated for many reasons. Part of what is confusing is that when we say "sugar," we are not talking about one ingredient. We really are talking about many ingredients that together make up the family of simple sugars. To complicate matters, it is the sugar that is added to foods that poses the most problems.

Glucose, sucrose, dextrose, and fructose are all in the family of simple sugars. They may have similar numbers of calories, but there are significant differences in how the body uses them. An example of this is the effect of a food on a person's blood glucose level as indicated by where it is on the glycemic index. Most important of all, each type has a unique impact on your desire to eat more. Here is a short rundown on these simple sugars.

Glucose is found circulating in your bloodstream. When you eat carbohydrates, your body converts them into glucose, and glucose is absorbed directly into your bloodstream. One of the important functions of glucose is to increase the secretion of the hormone insulin in your body. When you have insulin circulating in your blood, it signals to your brain that you have had enough to eat (satiety). This means that you are less likely to want more food.

Sucrose is the white sugar that is most familiar to most of us. It is usually made from sugar cane or sugar beets. The refined white sugar that is commonly used is 99.9 percent sucrose. When you consume products with sucrose, your body breaks it down into 50 percent glucose and 50 percent fructose. As a result, the level of glucose in your blood goes up.

Dextrose is a form of glucose that is made from the naturally occurring starch of certain plants, including corn, rice, wheat, potatoes, arrowroot, cassava, and sago. In the United States, most dextrose is made from cornstarch. To make dextrose, bacteria are fed cornstarch or some other starch. The bacteria then produce dextrose. Dextrose is used in many products ranging from intravenous (IV) preparations to baked goods. It has been judged to be 30 percent less sweet than sucrose.

Fructose is found in many plants (berries, root vegetables, sugar cane, flowers, fruits) and in honey. There is great variability in how much fructose and glucose is found in each type of fruit. Apples and pears have more fructose than apricots, while bananas have just about the same amount of fructose and glucose. Your body extracts the fructose from your blood stream and sends it to your liver. Fructose does not stimulate the release of insulin, which means that your brain does not get the signal that you have had enough to eat. It is 1.73 times as sweet as sucrose. In addition to fructose, fruit contains other nutrients.

High fructose corn syrup (HCFS) comes from corn. Cheaper than white sugar, HCFS is a manufactured product that has no nutritional value and also increases your appetite.

We need some sugar. The problem occurs when we eat too much of it, which has negative health consequences. This is now identified as a global health problem. In March 2015, WHO recommended that adults and children reduce their daily intake of free sugars to less than 10 percent of their total energy intake. WHO added that a further reduction to below 5 percent, or roughly 25 grams (6 teaspoons), per day would provide additional health benefits. In January, 2016, the United States released the 2015-2020 Dietary Guidelines for Americans, which encourage people to shift to having no more than 10 percent of their calories come from added sugars.

For a person eating 2000 calories a day, 10 percent means no more than 200 calories a day are from added sugar. This means that we have to be aware of how much sugar is in what we eat and drink. Take a close look at the Nutrition Facts on the label of a 12-ounce can of a sugar-sweetened beverage. It shows you how much of the total carbohydrates come from sugar per serving. So what does it mean if it has 140 calories and 39 grams of sugar? It means that what you are drinking has the equivalent of 8 teaspoons of sugar. In other words, you are nearly at your daily limit.

And that desire for something sweet is something that many of us have not even thought about. When I was little, the only time anyone mentioned sugar as a problem was with respect to your teeth. I remember being told that too much sugar would give you cavities. As the years passed, I heard of people having too much sugar in their blood and more conversations about diabetes. But overall, sugar was not a major concern because people were not eating that much sugar in their foods. In recent decades, though, the number of foods and drinks with added sugar has skyrocketed.

For both children and adults, consumption of sugar-sweetened beverages is connected with carrying excess weight.

In the past few decades, our consumption of sweeteners has increased in dramatic ways, and the consequences are still unfolding. While the industry continues to dodge the facts, we know for certain that consumption of sugar-sweetened drinks is associated with excess weight in children.[5] The evidence for adults clearly connects excess weight to diabetes.

Sugar and Its Relationship to Other Conditions. What was still to be documented was whether sugar influenced the health of adults in other ways. In one study, Quanhe Yang,[6,7] a researcher at the CDC's Division for Heart Disease and Stroke Prevention, and his colleagues wanted to look at the trends in how much sugar people ate or drank and to try to determine if there were any consequences that were particularly notable. To do this, they analyzed the data from the National Health and Nutrition Examination Survey (NHANES) from 1988 to 2010. The NHANES is a unique series of studies in which *actual* measurements and tests are taken of the thousands of volunteers throughout the country that are randomly selected to be in this survey.

Yang looked carefully at all the people who had been part of the study and found out which ones had died. It was not surprising when the research team discovered that adults in the United States had diets with more sugar than was considered necessary. What was most surprising and concerning was their conclusion: "we observed a significant relationship between added sugar consumption and increased risk for [cardiovascular disease] mortality."

The people who had more sugar in their diet were more likely to die sooner from cardiovascular disease.

It was not just about the extra calories; it was that somehow the extra sugar in their diet increased the likelihood that they were going to die sooner from some sort of cardiovascular disease.

Your Brain On Sugar. In the May, 2015 *Proceedings of the National Academy of Sciences*, Shan Luo and colleagues[8] examined how 24 healthy volunteers responded to having a drink that was sweetened with either fructose or glucose. The study focused on:

- how their brain responded to images of food;
- choices the volunteers made to either get a food reward immediately or a monetary reward later; and,
- changes in the insulin levels in their blood.

At the beginning of the study, the researchers made sure that all volunteers started with similar levels of hunger. Additionally, they made sure that all the volunteers rated both the glucose and fructose drinks as pleasant.

What they found was that glucose and fructose may both be sweet, but that the effect of fructose was to make the person hungrier.

Fructose not only did not satisfy the way that glucose did, but it also made the volunteers want to get more food and to get it faster. Those who had the fructose were also more willing to give up monetary incentives.

The buzz about high-fructose corn syrup (HFCS) is true.

Recently, the discussion about sugar and its negative consequences has focused on the high-fructose corn syrup that is added to beverages. You may not think much about high-fructose corn syrup (HFCS) as an ingredient, but it is in many of the foods we eat and in our drinks. HCFS also has an almost-immediate negative impact on our health.[9]

Kimber L. Stanhope, a research scientist at the University of California at Davis, and her colleagues[10] wanted to better understand the effects of HCFS. To do so, they were able to get 85 people to be in their study. Everyone in the study had blood tests at the beginning. They were then assigned to one of four groups to observe the effects of HFCS. Depending on the group to which they were assigned for the next two weeks, participants had drinks that were sweetened with either aspartame, 10 percent HFCS, 17.5 percent HFCS, or 25 percent HFCS.

After two weeks, the blood levels of all participants were tested again. The major conclusion was that after just two weeks, the HFCS drinks were having a negative effect. The groups that had more HFCS in their drinks had higher levels of bad cholesterol (LDL) and triglycerides. "It was a surprise that adding as little as the equivalent of a half-can of soda at breakfast, lunch, and dinner was enough to produce significant increases in risk factors for cardiovascular disease," said Stanhope. She added, "Our bodies respond to a relatively small increase in sugar, and that's important information."

About Carbohydrates. Our bodies also break carbohydrates down into sugar. Given the facts about how our bodies use sugar and its impact on how we eat, we need to revisit the foods we eat that are high in carbohydrates—bread, rice, pasta, potatoes, and cereal, to name a few. We need some carbohydrates, but we have to be very thoughtful about what we are eating.

When the carbohydrates we eat turn into sugar quickly, it is bad on many fronts. While it may give us a quick energy boost, the effect lasts only a short time. What happens is that you end up crashing and feeling less satisfied more quickly than with carbohydrates that are turned into sugar at a slower rate.

A good rule of thumb is that the whiter the carbohydrate, the faster it turns into sugar. So eat what is darker. What makes bread, rice, and pasta white is that they have been processed and as a result have lost some of the nutrition that helps slow down the conversion to sugar.

The solution is simple. When you eat carbohydrates, eat whole-grain bread, whole-wheat pasta, and brown rice. Applying the rule to potatoes means that is it better to eat sweet potatoes than white potatoes.

Whole grains make a positive difference to your health.

While it may make sense to eat whole grains, it was not until recently that there was a major effort to document the consequences of eating them. A group of researchers set out to look at the data collected from two huge studies that were designed to complement each other.[11] One of these studies was of women (The Nurses' Health Study) and the other was of men (Health Professionals Follow-Up Study).

The Nurses' Health Study (NHS) looked at what happens to the health of a large group of women over time. In the original study, the participants were 121,700 registered nurses who lived in eleven states and were 30 to 55 years old. The Health Professionals

Follow-Up Study looked at 51,529 men in health professions. In both studies, each participant receives questionnaires to answer about their health and health-related habits every two years.

After studying the answers to questionnaires and looking at when and why people died, the conclusion was that people who ate more whole grains were less likely to have cardiovascular problems. What was surprising was the consistency of this finding regardless of a person's lifestyle. Eating whole grains is good for us. Whole grains are carbohydrates, but they take a lot longer to be converted into sugar.

The Benefits of Eating Whole Fruit. Some of our need for sweet things in our diet is satisfied by the fruits we eat. While in our hurried life we may prefer the ease and speed of drinking juice, it is much better to eat the whole fruit, even when the juice is natural.

Think of fruit juice as processed fruit. The juice from fruit gets turned into sugar faster than when you eat the piece of fruit. When you drink juice instead of eating the whole fruit, you lose the nutrients and fiber that help slow down the absorption of the fructose (sugar) in the fruit. An additional benefit of eating fruit is that when you eat a piece of fruit, you will eat it slower and feel full longer.

Artificial sweeteners are not the solution.

The logical conclusion is to avoid sugar and just have artificial sweeteners. But that is not a good idea. The research is quite alarming: even though artificial sweeteners have fewer or no calories, you are still more likely to get diabetes.[12,13] When it comes to sugar, be thoughtful. A little bit is okay, but if you have too much you put yourself at considerable risk for diabetes and cardiovascular disease. Sugar also makes you want to eat even when you may not be hungry.

Fat

The message that fat is the enemy is misleading. In order to function well, the body needs some fat. Vitamins and nutrients usually need either fat or water to be absorbed. Vitamins that need fat in order to be absorbed are also the ones that your body stores. Fat-soluble vitamins include A, D, E, and K. As this list shows, they provide essential benefits.

Benefits of Select Vitamins[14]

<u>Vitamin A</u>   Helps form and maintain healthy skin, teeth, bones, soft tissue (such as tendons, ligaments, muscles), and mucus membranes. It also promotes good vision, especially in low light situations. It may also be needed for reproduction and breast-feeding.

<u>Vitamin D</u>   Helps your body absorb calcium. Calcium is one of the main building blocks of bone. Ten to 15 minutes of sunshine three times a week is enough to produce the body's requirement of vitamin D for most people at most latitudes. People who do not live in sunny places may not make enough vitamin D. Lack of vitamin D may also have a role in diabetes, hypertension, and autoimmune conditions such as multiple sclerosis.

<u>Vitamin E</u>   Helps protect cells from damage caused by compounds the body produces. It also helps the immune system. Cells use vitamin E for other important functions too. For example, it helps the body form red blood cells and use vitamin K.

<u>Vitamin K</u>   This is the name given to a family of compounds that have similar basic chemistry. Vitamin K is not listed among the essential vitamins, but without it blood would not clot (coagulate) properly. It is also needed so that bones and other tissues develop properly.

We need to eat some fat because fat helps us absorb vitamins and other nutrients that are essential for our health. What we need to be careful about is the type of fat we eat and how much of it we eat. The type of fat is very important.

In R. J. de Souza's[15] study of studies, the research team looked across a multitude of observational investigations to see if eating saturated fats or trans fats increased (1) all causes of death, (2) CVD, or (3) type 2 diabetes. The conclusion was that trans fats were associated with an increase in all causes of death, CVD, and type 2 diabetes. The exact opposite was found with saturated fats. Does this mean that you can eat all the butter you would like? Of course not.

That is why we have to understand the new changes in the dietary guidelines.

The 2015 Dietary Guidelines Advisory Committee (DGAC) report[16] made at least two changes of interest to all of us concerning the fat that we eat. First, cholesterol content in our food should not be a concern. This was based on the evidence that there was no meaningful link between the cholesterol in our food and what was measured in our blood. The second change was that instead of having a limit on the amount of fat we eat, it would be better to focus on the type of fat that we eat. Nuts, vegetable oils, and fish help our bodies work better and should be part of what we eat. When the 2015-2020 Dietary Guidelines for Americans were released, the message was clear: if we are thoughtful about the fats we eat, not only are they okay[17] but they are essential to our health. Not only are fats a source of energy, but they are essential so that the body can use some vitamins.

No to Any Artificial Trans Fat. What you must totally avoid is anything with artificial trans fat. Artificial trans fat does all the wrong things to your cardiovascular system: it lowers your good cholesterol (HDL) and raises both your bad cholesterol (LDL) and triglycerides. Where does artificial trans fat come from? Trans fat is made in a process that adds hydrogen to vegetable oil and is sometimes referred to as partially hydrogenated. Trans fats are often used because they make for a longer shelf life for baked goods, many kinds of chips, margarine, nondairy coffee creamer, and other foods. They are what makes ready-made frosting spreadable. They may save time when making frosting, and they may make for cheaper foods, but artificial trans fats are very bad for us.

The good news is that many makers of processed food are working to eliminate trans fats from their products. By 2018, most companies will not be allowed to add partially hydrogenated oils to their food.[18] In the meantime, it is best to read the list of ingredients on the food label. If the list includes partially hydrogenated vegetable oil, look for a different product. This situation will get easier as the FDA moves to eliminate trans fats from our food supply completely.

The key fact is that we still need some fat, and we need the good fats. The best fats are those that are unsaturated, either monounsaturated or polyunsaturated.[19, 20]

Monounsaturated Fat Sources	Omega-6 Polyunsaturated Fat Sources	Omega-3 Polyunsaturated Fat Sources
Nuts	Soybean oil	Soybean oil
Vegetable oils	Corn oil	Canola oil
Canola oil	Safflower oil	Walnuts
Olive oil		Flaxseed
High oleic safflower oil		Fish (trout, herring, and salmon
Sunflower oil		
Avocados		

You just have to be thoughtful and add these unsaturated fats to your foods in small amounts. I was sad to learn that a handful (of a relatively small hand) of walnuts measured only ¼ cup but had 160 calories, or about 10 percent of my caloric goal for the day.

Then there is the complicated situation with saturated fat. Saturated fat is usually in those very yummy high-fat cheeses, meats that have lots of fat (bacon, brisket, ribs, steaks that are nicely marbled), palm and coconut oil (used in many desserts), milk, cream, butter, and ice cream. We have to be very careful about how much of these we eat for a variety of reasons. What surprises many people is what may be hidden in the fat.

While saturated fat adds flavor and calories to what we eat, a growing concern is that harmful compounds can settle and accumulate in animal fat, which is then consumed by people.

For example, dioxins are compounds that, according to the WHO, "are highly toxic and can cause reproductive and developmental problems, damage the immune system, interfere with hormones, and also cause cancer."[21] According to the National Institute of Environmental Health Sciences (NIEHS) dioxins are the result of "incineration processes, including improper municipal waste incineration and burning of trash, and can be released into the air during natural processes, such as forest fires and volcanoes." What this means is that if dioxin is in the air it can then settle into the water and soil. The dioxin is then absorbed by plants. The dioxin then accumulates in the animals and fish that eat the plants that had absorbed the dioxin.

Once you eat food with dioxin, your body stores it. It accumulates, and the dioxin maintains at least half of its potency for seven to 11 years. NIEHS recommends that to reduce your exposure to dioxin, you should remove skin from fish and chicken, eat lean meats, and trim fat. When eating fresh-caught fish, be aware of limits that may have been placed on eating fish from a specific body of water, drink fat-free or low-fat milk, and use butter in moderation. Additionally, according to the FDA, "The highest concentration of dioxins in livestock, fish, and shellfish are typically found in fat and the liver."[22]

Other studies have found that when people and animals are exposed to dioxin early in life, it does more than raise their risk for cancer. It also increases the risk of cancer in the next generation. [23,24] But dioxin is not the only chemical substance in our environment to be concerned about.

There are other factors that may be changing how we eat and how our body uses what we eat. Our endocrine system produces hormones that affect everything from how we metabolize food to our sexual development.

When this system is not sending the right signal at the right time, many aspects of our lives can be upset. We now recognize that there are chemical substances that we have added to our environment that impact the hormones in our body. These substances are called endocrine-disrupting chemicals (EDCs), and they seem to have an effect on body weight.

Bisphenol A (BPA) is an EDC that increases the risk for metabolic disorders as well as for reaching puberty earlier than expected, which results in gaining weight.[25, 26, 27] This has a significant effect on how we use the food we eat and how fat accumulates in our body. We now know that EDCs, which are in many of the products that we use (shampoos, nail polish, cleaning products, plastics, etc.) change how our hormones work.

The connection to fat is summarized by endocrine researcher Andrea Gore and colleagues: "Fat is a particularly important reservoir for EDCs, as these chemicals' compositions tend to make them fat-soluble."[28] In other words, wherever there is accumulated fat, there are EDCs, and that just provides another reasons to avoid animal fat.[29]

In summary, there are many factors that influence how much we eat, what we eat, and how our body uses what we consume. There is no single food to avoid and no simple solution. That should not discourage you. Rather, it should keep you alert to the many considerations that make it difficult to manage your weight. There are many elements that play a role in the hard work of eating healthy. The challenge is to control as many as we can. At the very least, we should reduce how much added sugar is in what we eat and drink. When it comes to fat, we need to focus on the healthy sources of fat, and for many reasons we need to take the fat off the meat we eat. There should be no artificial trans fats in our food.

The bottom line is that there is much to incorporate into the decisions we make as to what we eat.

---

[1] Zeevi, D.; Korem, T.; Zmora, N.; Israeli. D.; Rothschild, D.; Weinberger, A.; Ben-Yacov, O.; Lador, D.; Avnit-Sagi, T.; Lotn-Pompan, M.; Suez, J.; et al. "Personalized Nutrition by Prediction of Glycemic Responses". *Cell*. Volume 163, Issue 5, 19 November 2015, Pgs. 1079-1094 DOI: http://dx.doi.org/10.1016/j.cell.2015.11.001

[2] Ley, R. E. "Obesity and the Human Microbiome," *Current Opinion in Gastroenterology*. 2010;26(1) Pgs. 5-11.

[3] Locke, A.E.; Kahali, B.; Berndt, S. I. et al. "Genetic studies of body mass index yield new insights for obesity biology," *Nature*, February 12, 2015, 518, Pgs.197-206 DOI: http://dx.doi.org/10.1038/nature14177

[4]   Claussnitzer, M.; Dankel, S. N.; Kim, K-H; Quon, G.; Meuleman, W.; Haugen, C.; Glunk, V.; Sousa, I. S.; Beaudry, J. L.; Puviindran, V.; Abdennur, N. A.; Liu, J.; Svensson, P-A.; Hsu, Y-H.; Drucker, D. J.; Mellgren, G.; Hui, C. C.; Hauner, H. and Kellis, M. "*FTO* Obesity Variant Circuitry and Adipocyte Browning in Humans," *New England Journal of Medicine*, August 19, 2015. DOI: http://dx.doi.org/10.1056/NEJMoa1502214

[5]   Ludwig, D.S.; Peterson, K.E. and Gortmaker, S.L. "Relation Between Consumption of Sugar-sweetened Drinks and Childhood Obesity: A Prospective, Observational Analysis," *The Lancet*. Vol 357, February 17, 2001. Pgs. 505-508.

[6]   Yang, Q.; Zhang, Z.; Gregg, E.W.; Flanders, W.; Merritt, R.; Hu, F.B. "Added Sugar Intake and Cardiovascular Diseases Mortality Among US Adults," *JAMA Internal Medicine*. 2014;174(4) Pgs. 516-524. DOI: http://dx.doi.org/10.1001/jamainternmed.2013.13563

[7]   Kearns, C.E.; Schmidt, L.A. and Glantz, S.A. Sugar Industry and Coronary Heart Disease Research: A Historical Analysis of Internal Industry Documents. Special Communication. Pages E1-6 *JAMA Internal Medicine*, Published online September 12, 2016

[8]   Luo, S.; Monterosso, J.R.; Sarpelleh, K. and Page, K.A. "Differential Effects of Fructose Versus Glucose on Brain and Appetitive Responses to Food Cues and Decisions for Food Rewards." *Proceedings of the National Academy of Sciences*. May 19, 2015, vol. 112, no. 20, Pgs. 6509–6514 before print May 4, 2015, DOI: http://dx.doi.org/10.1073/pnas.1503358112

[9]   Stanhope, K.L.; Medici, V.; Bremer, A.A.; Lee, V.; Lam, H.D.; Nunez, M.V.; Chen, G.X.; Keim, N.L. and Havel, P.J. "A Dose-response Study of Consuming High-fructose Corn Syrup–sweetened Beverages on Lipid/Lipoprotein Risk Factors for

Cardiovascular Disease in Young Adults. *American Journal of Clinical Nutrition*. First published ahead of print April 22, 2015 DOI: http://dx.doi.org/10.3945/ajcn.114.100461

10   Ibid.

11   Wu, H.; Flint, A.J.; Qi, Q.; van Dam, R.M.; Sampson, L.A.; Rimm, E. B.; Holmes, M.D.; Willett, W.C; Hu, F.B. and Sun, Q. "Association Between Dietary Whole Grain Intake and Risk of Mortality: Two Large Prospective Studies in US Men and Women." *JAMA Internal Medicine*. March 2015, Volume 175, Number 3, Pgs. 373-384.

12   Shell, E. R. "Artificial Sweeteners May Change our Gut Bacteria in Dangerous Ways." *Scientific American*. April 1, 2015

13   Jotham, S.T.; Korem, D.; Zeevi, G.; Zilberman-Schapira, C.A.; Thaiss, O.; Maza, D.; Israeli, N.; Zmora, S.; Gilad, A.; Weinberger, Y.; Kuperman, A.; Harmelin, I.; Kolodkin-Gal, H.; Shapiro, Z.; Halpern Eran, S. and Eran E.   "Artificial Sweeteners Induce Glucose Intolerance By Altering the Gut Bacteria." *Nature*. October 9, 2014 Vol. 514. Pgs. 181-198. DOI: http://dx.doi.org/10.1038/nature13793

14   "Vitamins." MedlinePlus Medical Encyclopedia. https://www.nlm.nih.gov/medlineplus/ency/article/002399.htm Updated February 2, 2015 by Emily Wax, RD, The Brooklyn Hospital Center, Brooklyn, NY. Also reviewed by David Zieve, MD, MHA, Isla Ogilvie, PhD, and the A.D.A.M. Editorial team.

15   de Souza, R. J.; Mente, A.; Maroleanu, A.; Cozma, A. I.; Ha, V.; Kishibe, T.; Uleryk, E.; Budylowski, P.; Schünerman, H.; Beyene, J. and Anand, S. S. "Intake of Saturated and Trans Unsaturated Fatty Acids and Risk of All-Cause Mortality, Cardiovascular Disease, and Type 2 Diabetes: Systematic Review and Meta-analysis of Observational Studies." *BMJ* 2015; 351.

DOI: http://dx.doi.org/10.1136/bmj.h3978 (Published 12 August 2015)

[16]   Dietary Guidelines Advisory Committee, "Scientific Report of the 2015 Dietary Guidelines Advisory Committee." 2015. http://www.health.gov/dietary guidelines/2015-scientific-report/. Accessed March 25, 2015.

[17]   Mozaffarian, D. and Ludwig, D.S. "The 2015 US Dietary Guidelines: Lifting the Ban on Total Dietary Fat," *JAMA*. 2015; 313(24) Pgs. 2421- 2422. DOI: http://dx.doi.org/10.1001/jama.2015.5941

[18]   "Dietary Fats." Medline Plus Medical Encyclopedia. https://www.nlm.nih.gov/medlineplus/dietaryfats.html Page last updated February 8, 2016 Topic Last reviewed March 25, 2015.

[19]   "Polyunsaturated Fats and Monounsaturated Fats," Nutrition for Everyone. Centers for Disease Control and Prevention. http://www.cdc.gov/nutrition/everyone/basics/fat/unsaturated fat.html

[20]   Wang, D.D.; Li, Y.; Chiuve, S.E.; Stampfer, M.J.; Manson, J.E.; Rimm, E.B.; Willett, W.C. and Hu, F.B. "Association of Specific Dietary Fats with Total and Cause-Specific Mortality." *JAMA Intern Med.* doi: http://dx.doi.org/10.1001/jamainternmed.2016.2417 Published online July 5, 2016.

[21]   "Dioxins and Their Effects on Human Health." Factsheet No. 225. World Health Organization. Updated June 2014. http://www.who.int/mediacentre/factsheets/fs225/en/

[22]   "Questions & Answers About Dioxins and Food Safety," Food and Drug Administration. February 2012. Updated

06/19/2013
http://www.fda.gov/Food/FoodborneIllnessContaminants/Che
micalContaminants/ucm077524.html

23   Mead, N.M. "Cancer Collusion? Dietary Fat May Modify
Dioxin- Induced Mammary Cancer Risk," *Environmental Health
Perspectives* 118:a217-a217 (2010) DOI: http://dx.doi.org/
10.1289/ehp.118-a217b [online 01 May 2010].

24   Merrill, M.L.; Harper, R.; Birnbaum, L.S.; Cardiff, R.D. and
Threadgill, D.W. "Maternal Dioxin Exposure Combined with a
Diet High in Fat Increases Mammary Cancer Incidence in Mice,"
Environmental Health Perspectives 118:596-601 (2010). DOI:
http://dx.doi.org/10.1289/ehp.0901047 [online 09 December
2009]

25   vom Saal, F.S. and Myers, J.P . "Bisphenol A and Risk of
Metabolic Disorders," *JAMA*, September 17, 2008. Vol 300,
No.11 Pgs. 1353- 1355.

26   Lang, I.A.; Galloway T.S.; Scarlett, A.; Henley, W. E.;
Depledge, M.; Wallace, R.B. and Melzer, D. "Association of
Urinary Bisphenol: A Concentration with Medical Disorders and
Laboratory Abnormalities in Adults. *JAMA*. 2008; 300(11) Pgs.
1303-1310.

27   Richter, C.A.; Birnbaum, L.S.; Farabollini, F.; Newbold, R.R.;
Rubin, B.S.; Talsness, C.E.; Vandenbergh, J.G.; Walser-Kuntz, D.
R. and von Saal, F.S. "*In Vivo* Effects of Bisphenol A in
Laboratory Rodent Studies. *Reproductive Toxicology*. 2007; 24(2)
Pgs. 199-224.

28   Gore, A.C.; Crews, D.; Doan, L.L.; Merrill, M.L.; Patisual, H.
and Zota, A. "Introduction to Endocrine Disrupting Chemicals
(EDCs): A Guide for Public Interest Organizations and
Policymakers." *Endocrine Society*. December 2014. Pg. 16.

[29] "Dioxins and Dioxin-like Compounds in the Food Supply: Strategies to Decrease Exposure." Committee on the Implications of Dioxin in the Food Supply, National Research Council http://www.nap.edu/catalog/10763.html

CHAPTER 5
Winning Strategies

I knew that I had to change how, when, and what I would eat. I found that this was part of the realignment I had to do to eat in a healthy way. How was I going to make it through the day, given that my days are hectic and unpredictable? I had to come up with a strategy that would work for myself and that others could use.

It was interesting to read about celebrities who had staff to prepare their foods, but few of us have a chef at home. So how to eat in a healthy way to manage my weight was a challenge when I also had to cook for my family. I soon realized that if I ate in a healthier way, so would everyone else. I came up with some simple rules to help guide what I would do when it came to food and my weight.

These strategies made the changes easier. Notice that I use the word "easier" rather than "easy." I know that there is nothing easy about changing what you do or how you think. This is tough, because we often think or act without pausing to consider the consequences. And now I had to stop and think about what I was doing so that I could recognize and embrace my mild hunger. It takes a considerable amount of attentiveness and focus to be aware of the social and bodily cues that drive you to eat. And you have to do this even when you do not feel like thinking about what you are doing.

What I followed were my four strategies for healthier eating: pleasure, portion, process, and patience. This helped me change how I thought about what and how much I ate and drank. Once I accepted this new way of thinking, I could make it through the day. These are the healthy eating strategies that we all need to develop.

Pleasure

Food is not my enemy. Chocolate, for example, is a food that we can enjoy in small amounts.[1] And I fully and deeply enjoy eating a piece of dark chocolate, especially when it is more than 70 percent cacao. I am one of those people who did a celebratory dance when research pointed out the benefits of dark chocolate. I love the way chocolate smells and how it feels when I bite into it. Chocolate coats my tongue with flavors that go down my throat, and fills a special place that brings a smile to my face.

I may have to think about what and how much I eat, but I also celebrate the fact that I like to eat and enjoy food. If I was going to eat something I was going to enjoy eating it. Given that I was now limiting the amount of food I ate in one day I was not going to waste my calories on food that was not tasty. I wasn't going to eat something just because the food was in front of me, free, or because everyone else was eating.

Whenever I ate, I was going to savor the food. Pleasure takes time, and eating had to be allocated a reasonable amount of time. I was not going to pop food into my mouth and chew it mindlessly while I was getting ready to pop the next piece in my mouth. The pleasure of eating means giving yourself the time to taste the flavors. If you do not have the time to enjoy your food, then take it as an opportunity to eat less. Avoid eating fast. It diminishes the experience of eating and undermines the ability of your body and brain to connect and let you know that you are full. I told myself that speed-eating is the enemy of eating in a healthy manner. I knew this from what others had shared with me and through what I had observed.

Eating slowly helps you be less hungry.

There is a lot of research to support the importance of eating slowly. Eric Robinson,[2] a researcher from the

Departments of Psychological Sciences (ER) and Biostatistics (CTS and SJN), University of Liverpool, and his colleagues wanted to review all of the existing experiments in which how fast someone ate was varied to see the effect, if any, on how much people ate or on how hungry they felt. They focused on 22 studies that met their research criteria. The analysis across all the studies found that the people who ate slower ate less. Eating slowly helps you be less hungry.

The key takeaway from all the studies is that to eat less, you should eat slowly. But how do you do that when we live in a society that is geared to speed eating? Robinson and his colleagues did not give a specific technique for how to get someone to eat slowly. Instead, they stated that "to reduce eating rate deserves attention both in a clinical and public health context." The importance of pleasure when you eat is conveyed by their statement that "A fast eating rate is directly related to a lower duration of sensory exposure per unit (in g or kcal) of food." Eating slow gives our senses more opportunity to have pleasure as we eat.

So how slow is slow? It depends on you and what you are eating. I am not going to say how many times you should chew in a minute or a mouthful. A better gauge is to watch how long it takes you to eat a meal. If you pile your plate high (even if it's salad without dressing) and wolf it down in under 10 minutes, you are undermining your efforts to eat healthily. Remember: it's about pleasure, not speed.

Part of the pleasure of eating also requires that you eat because your body needs nutrition and not because eating has become a vector for dealing with stress, which has been proven not to be a healthy practice. There is evidence that when you eat because you are stressed, you are less sensitive to your own hunger or to feelings of fullness.[3] In other words, when you eat when stressed, you end up eating more. And we all know how easy it is for that to happen.

Countless people have told me that they were sitting with a bowl of chips nearby and before they knew it, the bowl was empty. The chips had not evaporated; each person had eaten all of the chips because they were engrossed in what they were watching, or were feeling nervous, sad, or depressed, or were experiencing some other feeling. They were not even noticing how much they were eating. Eating for pleasure means eating slowly and being aware of your food.

Eating and multitasking is not a good combination. If it is time to eat a meal, you should eat. That does not mean that you have to stop all conversation. Obviously, when your mouth is full you will not be talking, but the corollary for managing how and what you eat is that when someone else is talking you should not be eating. There is a limit to how many channels your brain can process at one time. It is difficult to fully listen to someone and savor your food at the same time. That is why to fully enjoy your food, when someone is speaking put your fork down and listen. You will be a better listener, and you will also give your stomach time to tell your brain that you are starting to get full.

Sometimes, of course, you will have to eat quickly because you are short on time and beyond mild hunger. Those are times when you have to be prepared with something quick, nutritious, and easy to eat that is satisfying. This could be a piece of fruit, a pickle, a carrot, or a small piece of dark chocolate. I discovered that for me, a madeleine, a very small sponge cake with a distinctive shell-like shape, with its one hundred calories was the best way to reduce my feelings of hunger to a manageable "desiring food" level and still stay within my sugar limit for the day. And I could also carry one madeleine in my purse if I needed to nibble until my next meal. It was small enough to savor and tasty enough to satisfy. I taught myself to satisfy my taste buds and save my calories for when I would have the time to slow down and enjoy a real meal.

Each one of us has to find what can satisfy us in a way that is healthy and fulfilling. The goal is always to enjoy what you eat and not to just speed-eat or stuff yourself.

Portion

Our thoughts about portion size are intertwined with our personal history. If you are from a large family, your view of portion can range from "let me take a small piece so everyone can have some" to "I'll take everything I can now because there will not be enough for seconds." In other homes, a small portion is associated with lack of available food, a limited budget, or frugality.

For persons from a modest or immigrant background, abundance of food is a reflection of success: it means that you have made it. Serving large amounts of food communicates that you are successful, able to provide for yourself and others, and that you are no longer hungry. It is not just about eating the food you want but having leftovers or excess. The existence of a "doggy bag" is not a universal part of eating out. Likewise, "supersize it" is not just a marketing strategy— it is part of the "more is better" cultural imperative.

All this makes it difficult to eat or serve smaller portions. The fact is, most portions are more than is necessary for most people to get full. This is very problematic, because if you are served more, you will eat more. This is called the portion-size effect (PSE). While we know it is true, the reasons we eat more remain unclear.[4]

I found that the best way to begin was to know how much food I was actually eating and what a portion would be for me. I know that the labels on products provide valuable information about nutrition, but when it came to portion size, they were sometimes off the mark. For example, a small (4.375 ounces or 125 grams) can of sardines packed in marinara sauce was one portion for me, but on the label it was listed as being 2.5 servings. The important lesson was that sometimes there was a mismatch between what was a portion for me and what was listed as a serving size. So how was I to determine what was right for me?

In order to know how much was a reasonable portion, I did three things. First I bought a small digital scale online. Including shipping, it cost under $20. Second, I took out my measuring cup and spoons and put them by the table next to my new scale. Then I began to measure everything I ate at home so I could determine the number of calories and how much it would be reasonable to eat at a meal.

The initial findings were sobering. I quickly and sadly learned that a cup of pasta or rice (and that meant being honest and not packing it into the measuring cup) is less food that I thought. Actually, it was a lot less than what I thought. I tried different shapes of pasta, but it was still less. The same when I measured rice or mashed potatoes. The conclusion was that my portions of pasta, rice, or potatoes had to become much smaller.

As I watch people fill their plates at a salad bar I can see how the 50 calories in a green leafy salad gets amped up with so many more calories by adding a few of the usual optional items. Just modestly adding ½ cup kidney beans (110 calories), ¼ cup bacon bits (100 calories), and ¼ cup salad dressing (100 calories) transforms the 50- calorie salad to a 360-calorie one. Then, when you add drinks and the rest of the lunch, you are probably close to the typical person's daily caloric limit.

This ramping up of calories is compounded by the fact that everything is larger than necessary. It is not just the beverages with added sweeteners that are oversized. Sandwiches and rolls are so huge that by themselves they take an unreasonable chunk out of your daily calorie limit. Once you add a little mayonnaise (one tablespoon is actually not enough to adequately cover a slice of bread), there are no calories left for whatever else you were going to put in the sandwich. To make matters worse, since few people have flexible work schedules, there is no time for additional exercise to try to balance the calories in the sandwich you just inhaled because you were rushing to get back to your daily tasks.

When it comes to food and portions, you have to start by measuring to know how much you are actually eating. It will amaze you; it still amazes me.

Process

I understand that we all love certain tastes. The food science is clear that we like sweet things. We also like food that makes us feel good. In order to eat less, I knew I had to eat those food items that helped me. I quickly learned that the best products were the ones that were less processed.

When I am not home, the choices of unprocessed food are either nonexistent or unpalatable. Whether on the street, at the airport, or in a mall, the healthy options are just not there. The fast food or quick service places capture your interest with their easy-to-grab and easy-on-the-pocket options. But even the food that is relatively low in calories is typically doused with too much salt (which makes you drink more), high fructose corn syrup (which makes you feel hungry), and an assortment of high calorie trimmings, sauces, oils, and other high calorie items. It is a challenge to eat a healthy meal even when you pick the broiled chicken or the salad, because all the sides that you are encouraged to add do not help. And forget about French fries; they are not worth the calories.

It is not that processing is bad, or that everything natural is good. I remind myself that arsenic is natural but not good. One of the concerns with foods that are processed is all the ingredients that are added, and sometimes the actual processing itself does not help. I also found that most foods had too much sodium. Besides all the concerns about having too much sodium in my diet, I found that the foods loaded with sodium made me retain water. Also, when a label said natural, I had no idea what that actually meant.

I decided that to eat healthy and save money, I would make my own food and buy food that was in season or on sale. This was an easy way to vary what I ate. I learned to appreciate that what was in season is tastier, fresher, and less expensive. I could successfully control the quality and the portions of what I ate by using real food and ingredients. My freezer became my best friend.

My rule of thumb for healthy eating is to stick to products whose ingredients I can pronounce, or at least recognize.

Patience

IWWIWWIWI, which stands for "I want what I want when I want it," is the theme of too many of our lives. Somehow our daily life has evolved to a point that whatever we want, we want immediately. Most of the services that have grown around us are geared to making things happen quickly. Amazon has grown because they deliver within two days, and sometimes within hours. We do all we can to avoid or shorten lines. Not waiting is the goal.

When it comes to developing new eating behaviors, we have to learn to be patient. That means waiting. This is not just about eating slowly. The goals that we work towards are only reasonable if we give ourselves the time to achieve them. Moreover, eating healthy is a practice that will be with us for as long as we live. It is a part of our life journey.

The key is to find the combination of strategies that works for you so that you can appreciate mild hunger, enjoy what you eat, and know the value of what you eat for the rest of your life.

Eating Strategies

Do not eat based on what other people are eating. You have to eat for your needs and pleasure. Others may choose to eat more or less than you do. The biggest mistake I see is when people serve themselves the same amount that they see someone else put on a plate. People's bodies use food in very different ways. The research that I discussed earlier tells us that two people eating the same food can have very different outcomes with respect to how their body uses the food. This is especially the case when men are compared with women. Men actually need to eat more food than women do.

Measure your food. When you eat at home it is good to keep a food scale and measuring spoons and cups near where you eat. This will help increase the accuracy of your judgment in estimating the size of your portion when you are elsewhere. This also helps you to learn how many calories you are really eating. To say the least this was an area where I learned how much I really ate. It was much more than I thought. A cup of pasta sounds like a lot but it really is not. Most restaurant servings are about 2 cups. If you add some tomato sauce and a little bit of grated cheese your pasta is about 600 calories.

Find your food bliss. Previously I fessed up to the satisfaction and magic of madeleines. I also like ice cream; a little bit is very satisfying. Having both of these treats when I wanted them helped keep me on track. At about 100 calories each, they were better and less expensive than all the prepared 100-calorie snacks from grocery stores. And they were so much more satisfying.

Plan for treats. Of course, there are some foods that we know have a lot of calories. That just means that every now and then we have to adjust our calorie intake and activities so that we can indulge ourselves. I feel that way about pizza. I enjoy it and I do not want to give it up completely. Every now and then I plan for it. I know that a New York–style plain slice of pizza has about 300 calories and that I eat two slices. So I eat less that day or increase my activity for the day and allow myself to desire that pizza. When I eat my two slices of pizza I do not devour them; I savor and relish each bite.

1   Golomb, B.A.; Koperski, S. and, White, H.L. "Association Between More Frequent Chocolate Consumption and Lower Body Mass Index." *Archives of Internal Medicine.* Vol 172 (No.6) March 26, 2012. Pgs. 519-521.

2   Robinson, E.; Almiron-Roig, E.; Rutters, F.; de Graaf, C.; Forde, C. G.; Tudur Smith, C.; Nolan, S. J. and Jebb, S. A. "A Systematic Review and Meta-analysis Examining the Effect of Eating Rate on Energy Intake and Hunger." *American Journal Clinical Nutrition,* 2014;100, Pgs.123–51.

3   Tan, C. C. and Chow, C. M. "Stress and Emotional Eating: The Mediating Role of Eating Dysregulation," *Personality and Individual Differences,* Vol 66, Aug 2014, 1-4. DOI: http://dx.doi.org/10.1016/j.paid.2014.02.033

4   Herman, C.P.; Polivy, J.; Pliner, P. and Vartanian, L. R. "Mechanisms Underlying the Portion-size Effect," *Physiology & Behavior,* Vol 144, May 2015, 129-136. DOI: http://dx.doi.org/10.1016/j.physbeh.2015.03.025

CHAPTER 6
How to Eat and Exercise

When I looked at what was available on weight management, I found that that the most widely-read ones were written by physicians, nutritionists, dieticians, or other health experts. They apply their craft and valuable experiences to form a strategy or plan to help people maintain a healthy weight. Nevertheless, the sound scientific principles that are often used to frame each approach seem to have at best limited benefit. Each approach takes people just so far before they slide back to where they started. It is not a yo-yo. It's a boomerang.

I discussed with my friend Alan the concept of mild hunger and how it was important in order to manage your weight. His response was adamant and predictable:
Alan: I don't want to be hungry.
Me: It is what you have to learn to do to really lose weight.
Alan: I lost weight on the coffee and popcorn diet. I did that for weeks.
Me: Yes, you lost weight and then you gained back everything you lost.

When it comes to the mechanics of what to do to manage your weight, it has always involved some combination of modifying what you eat and exercising more.

Eating

The many options that are available to get a person to eat in a different way and increase activity cover a broad range of possibilities. Some programs restrict you to 1,000 calories a day or less, others tell you to focus on eating foods low in carbohydrate, and others offer a magic pill to make you lose weight.

And while each strategy or plan may have some parts that are helpful for you, the fact is that within two years most people who follow any of these plans gain the weight back and often a little extra. There are many studies on weight loss that document this boomerang effect of weight gain. I know how very true the weight-gain boomerang is, because I have experienced it many times. As a behavioral scientist, researcher, and advocate I knew that there had to be a better way.

As I reviewed the different plans, I was stunned to realize that I had attempted so many of them. From Atkins to Fasting to South Beach to Grapefruit, I had tried a variety of plans. I would achieve some measure of success. Then, after a few months, I found myself putting back on the pounds I had lost.

I could not help but grin when I would hear the weight loss experts with all their credentials tell me that I just needed to try a bit harder. I was trying hard, but what they recommended did not provide a long-term solution that worked for me.

Perhaps the problem was also with how the people who were supposed to be helpful felt about the people with excess weight. Would you take your child to a pediatrician who does not like children? Of course not. Yet more often than you would think, the very people who are supposed to be helpful have a negative view of the people they are supposed to be helping. In a survey of 187 members of the British Dietetic Association, the dieticians viewed both overweight and obese people as being responsible for their excess weight. Even more troubling, the dietitians rated obese people more negatively than overweight people.[1]

In another study, researchers looked at data across fourteen independent databases and 10,043 respondents. They wanted to understand the attitudes of health professionals toward weight management. These attitudes were classified under eight attitude indicators. The findings showed that health professionals of normal weight were more likely to be more confident in their weight management practice, perceive fewer barriers to weight management, have more positive outcome expectations, have stronger role identity, and have more negative attitudes toward obese individuals than health professionals who were overweight or obese.[2] It can't be good that the very people that are supposed to help us do not appreciate our struggle.

But the basic challenge for each one of us is to discover what eating strategy works best for us. That is why Dr. Frank Sacks, Professor of Cardiovascular Disease Prevention in the Department of Nutrition, Harvard School of Public Health and his colleague[3] tried to decipher if there was a type of ideal formula for the percentage of fats, proteins, and carbohydrates to lose weight. In their study they were able to enlist 811 adults over a two-year period that agreed to modify what they eat.

Each person who was included in the study had a BMI under 40, did not have diabetes or heart problems, and was not taking any medicines that affected their weight. Based on an interview and questionnaire, it was determined that people who were in the study were motivated to lose weight.

These highly motivated individuals were assigned to one of four diets. They avoided using any popular or commercial names for each diet so as not to bias the volunteers. Instead the four diets were described as:

- low-fat, average-protein (20 percent fat, 15 percent protein, 65 percent carbs);
- low-fat, high-protein (20 percent fat, 25 percent protein, 55 percent carbs);
- high-fat, average-protein (40 percent fat, 15 percent protein, 45 percent carbs); or
- high-fat, high-protein (40 percent fat, 25 percent protein, 35 percent carbs).

Each person was also given the opportunity to participate in group or individual sessions throughout the two years of the study. Levels of physical activity were similar across all four groups.

The good news was that most (80 percent) of the people completed the study. Additionally, after six months, most people had lost about fourteen pounds, or 7 percent of their weight. Keeping the weight they had lost off was very challenging, and after twelve months, most people began to gain some of the weight back. What was most interesting was that "satiety, hunger, satisfaction with the diet, and attendance at group sessions were similar for all diets." In other words, regardless of which diet was followed, the people were having similar experiences and losing weight. And people who attended the group sessions were more likely to lose weight.

Sacks and his colleagues also measured each person's waist and found that there was no meaningful difference in waist size among the four groups. But the most important finding was that at the end of six months, and again when measured after two years, all participants had decreased their risk factors for cardiovascular disease and diabetes.

A major conclusion from the study was that any "type of diet, when taught for the purpose of weight loss with enthusiasm and persistence, can be effective." Obviously, changing how the people ate had been good for them, and it did not matter which diet they were on. What did help was sticking to it and being positive. It was all about adopting a new approach and sticking to it.

Although there are many commercial or proprietary programs to lose weight, it has been difficult to know which one is the best. They all have very seductive ads. Many have "before" and "after" pictures that show how well the program works.

Dr. Kimberly Gudzune, an assistant professor of medicine and a weight-loss specialist at the Johns Hopkins University School of Medicine, and her team[4] recently looked into the array of programs to see what they could decipher. They began by making a list of all the programs they could find. They ended up with 141 different programs. They narrowed the list to 32 programs by eliminating programs that were either not found throughout the United States, encouraged use of a particular medication or supplement, or required that you live in a special facility. The 32 programs involved either groups, very-low calorie meals, or self-directed programs. They obtained and evaluated 4,212 citations on those programs and independently reviewed everything they found.

Their carefully worded conclusion was that "clinicians could consider referring overweight or obese patients to Weight Watchers or Jenny Craig." Additionally, in Table 1 of their study they list the monthly costs of programs. Weight Watchers was at the low end ($43 a month) and Jenny Craig was at the upper end ($570 a month). What was encouraging was their statement that "our findings show that Weight Watchers participants consistently have greater weight loss than control/education participants and sustain it beyond twelve months."

I know people who have been very successful with Weight Watchers, but the challenge has always been the same. How can people maintain the weight that they have struggled to achieve? For me, Weight Watchers was not a program that I could fit into my unpredictable schedule. I tried other approaches, and, as was typical, I blamed myself when a plan that seemed to work for others was a total failure for me.

Finding The Best Plan.

I was trying to better understand the reason why some people were successful in one type of program while others were not when I came across the 2015 study by Drs. Martin Reinhardt and Susanne Votruba.[5] These researchers at the Phoenix Epidemiology and Clinical Research Branch (PECRB) conducted very intensive research on twelve people who had excess weight. They began by measuring how much energy they burned after a day of fasting. Keeping this information to themselves, the research proceeded to the next phase.

All the volunteers then spent 11 weeks in an inpatient setting at the Obesity and Diabetes Clinical Research Section of the National Institute of Diabetes and Digestive and Kidney Diseases in Phoenix. In that setting, they were limited to mostly sedentary activity and were asked not to exercise. Additionally, everything they ate was controlled. For the first three weeks, volunteers ate a standard weight-maintaining diet (WMD) with the number of calories determined by their weight and their sex. The food they ate was 50 percent carbohydrate, 30 percent fat, and 20 percent protein.

After this, for the next six weeks volunteers drank a liquid diet that had half the calories they usually consumed.

For the last two weeks, volunteers were again given a standard 100 percent WMD, but this time it was based on their new weight.

The results ended up showing what I always knew in my heart, had seen with my friends, and experienced. Even when you controlled for factors of age, race, gender, and baseline weight, the data suggested that there were two kinds of people. Some had a metabolism that was thrifty and others had a metabolism that was spendthrift. The thrifty people had a metabolism that slowed down after fasting. The spendthrifts had a metabolism that did not slow down after fasting.

Whether a person was thrifty or a spendthrift determined how much weight a person lost. Votruba's conclusion was that "while behavioral factors such as adherence to diet affect weight loss to an extent, our study suggests we should consider a larger picture that includes individual physiology–and that weight loss is one situation where being thrifty doesn't pay."

So how do you choose what eating plan to follow? There are so many choices that it is hard to decide. Judy Rodriguez's book The Diet Selector[6] provides valuable and succinct information on 50 popular weight-loss diets and 25 health-promotion and/or disease management diets. The At-A-Glance Evaluation Guide helps you decide which plan resonates with you.

While some of these plans are only intended for the short term, others are more for a life-long change. What is unique about this book is that it is easy to see the variety of options that are available to manage a person's weight. Just remind yourself that the purpose of food is to provide nutrition for every part of your body. More insight into how to eat was provided by a 2015 study conducted by clinical researchers at the National Institutes of Health in Bethesda, Maryland.

In August 2015, the headline was "NIH Study: Low-Fat Diet Better Than Low-Carb For Weight Reduction."[7] As is too often the case, the headline missed the key point. This study looked at 10 men and nine women who agreed to be placed on a restricted diet and live at the NIH Clinical Center while on the restricted diet. Each person agreed to spend two weeks at the Center, go home for a two-to-four week period, and then return for another two-week period. During each two- week session, each person ate either a low-fat or low-carb diet. When participants returned for the second two-week period, they received the other diet. During the time the people were in residence at the Center they exercised for one hour on a treadmill at a predetermined pace. Additionally, when they were in residence they would spend five days in a metabolic chamber. After all this, Hall noted, "it is likely more important to choose a diet that leads to a reduction in calorie intake that can be sustained for long periods of time."[8] In other words, pick a way of eating that will be with you for the rest of your life.

Add to this the conclusions from a recent study that looked at the glucose levels of 800 people every week and their response to 46,898 meals.[9] They found that even when people ate the same foods, their bodies did not respond in the same way. In fact, what they found was great variability. Their conclusion was that having the same dietary guidelines for everyone may not be as useful as was assumed. The best eating plan is tailored and personalized for you.

In addition to what we eat, we also have to be thoughtful about what we drink. We all need a better understanding of our body and of hydration. At a basic level, we need to be hydrated to provide water for our cells, because our cells are mostly water. Additionally, most of the chemical reactions that occur within our cells require water. This is also true for our overall metabolism. Moreover, for the systems in our body to properly extract, use, and store the nutrients in our food we need to have water. That is why water is key to our health. It also explains why all hydration is not the same. (The only people who say that all hydration is the same are the ones who are trying to sell us a product we should avoid.) If you want to stay hydrated, the easiest and least expensive choice is to drink water.

The best plan is the one that works for you, not just in the short run but for the rest of your life. In my plan, I ate whatever I wanted to eat; I just ate less. Some of the best healthy eating tips are:

Counting calories helps. It's a good way to know the value of what you are eating in terms of nutrition and energy.

Eat your nutrients. While supplements and vitamins are often recommended, keep in mind that your body may not absorb them as well. Dietary supplement companies, unlike drug companies, do not have to prove to the Food and Drug Administration (FDA) that their products are safe or effective.[10] These products may make claims of natural and safe benefits, but dietary supplement users' experiences may be different from what the label promised. Multiple studies have found that more than half of the products contain ingredients not listed on the label. These unknown ingredients may result in dangerous drug interactions or severe allergic reactions.[11, 12]

Avoid drinks with alcohol. About 5 ounces of wine, 1½ ounces of alcohol, or 8 ounces of beer has about 100 calories. Your typical drink is larger than that, and your typical mixed drink has about 300 calories. When you avoid alcohol, you save calories that have no nutritional value, and you also save money. Your liver will also appreciate your decision.

Eat slowly. It takes the stomach a while to digest, and even longer for the brain to recognize fullness. By eating slowly, you give your brain time to acknowledge when you are full. If eating slowly is totally out of the question, then begin your meal by eating a few low calorie favorites.

Drink lots of water. Remember, your cells need water to perform most of their work.

Eat a little protein. Think of protein as your long-acting morsel of satisfaction. When I initially cut back on how much I ate, I found that two ounces of ham at lunch would keep me satisfied till my afternoon snack.

Eat a piece of fruit instead of drinking juice. Drinking juice, regardless of how natural it is, is less desirable than eating a piece of fruit. When you eat a piece of fruit you eat it slower, have time to savor it, and get the goodness of the fiber.

Melons are great. I thought I did not like melons until I realized that what I do not like are unripe melons. Too often, what is available pre-cut in a grocery store or served in a restaurant are flavorless pieces, more like tasteless rocks than ripe melons. Melons are low in calories, sweet, and I found them very satisfying. You may find that leaving some cut up in the fridge is best. The only downside is that they are filled with water, and as a result you will have to empty your bladder more frequently.

Use balsamic vinegar (aged). This thick syrupy kind of vinegar is so flavorful that a little bit on a salad goes a long way. The bonus is that you do not have to use olive oil, and it covers the salad very well.

Ketchup and mustard are better than mayonnaise.

Red sauce is best. When you eat pasta have it with a tomato sauce instead of a white sauce. And while I love olive oil with bits of garlic, I know I have to be very careful. Each tablespoon of olive oil has 100 calories. And a tablespoon is very, very little.

Serve yourself rice and pasta in ½ cup increments. I love rice, but was surprised to find that my typical serving amounted to 2 cups of brown rice. If

I added to that 1 cup of beans, I was eating nearly 700 calories. As for pasta, it is eye-opening to see how much is in one cup.

Exercising is Essential

We all know the importance of moving more, regardless of how physically active our daily life may be. I work very hard at trying to move more. It is difficult, but I have learned that it has a significant positive impact on my overall wellness. Even the research shows that when people exercise it improves their quality of life even when their weight does not change.[13]

Knowing how important it is, I realized that adding more movement to my life seemed to have a different effect on me than on other people. And the studies supported my experience. Whether looking at the findings in teenagers[14] or in older persons, the research showed that having people do the same activity would not result in the same outcome.

This was demonstrated in a recent study that looked at the effect of exercise on older persons who led a sedentary life. The study included 95 sedentary men and women, ages 65 to 79. They all participated in one of two exercise programs. Each program lasted five months, with four days a week of aerobic training or three days a week of resistance training. The major finding was that even when people were doing the same exercises, the effects varied. The level of improvement varied by person. Some did not improve.[15]

Movement is good for many reasons that go beyond helping you to manage your weight. Take as an example the many benefits of tai chi. While it may look like you are just stretching, your body is responding in many other ways that we are just starting to learn to measure and document. According to the National Center for Complementary and Integrative Health, which is part of the National Institutes of Health, "There is some evidence to suggest that practicing tai chi may help people manage chronic pain associated with knee osteoarthritis and fibromyalgia."[16]

To make sure you move more, keep in mind the following:

Walking is wonderful. This is movement that most of us can do throughout our lives. You don't have to go fast; you just have to do as much as you can do and then slowly do more. The distance, speed, and terrain will change as your fitness level changes. You may think you do not have to time to go for a walk, but we can all incorporate more walking in our daily lives so easily.

Some examples include:

- 🐾 Hand deliver something to a co-worker rather than emailing it to them if they are nearby.
- 🐾 Take the stairs instead of the elevator if you are only going up a floor or two.
- 🐾 Don't take the closest parking to the entrance of your location.
- 🐾 When bringing in groceries, carry less and make more trips.

Do what you can do. Don't do something just because other people do it. It is wonderful when you have friends that can run a marathon or get into those incredible positions in yoga. You need to find the activities that you can do without injuring yourself. You have to be especially careful when taking part in a group activity. Focus on what you can do at this point in your life. Do not compare yourself to others or to what you were able to do before. Focus on doing what you can do now.

Track when and how much you move. You need to determine if you are a morning or evening person. For me, at the end of the day I am too tired. Although my work is sedentary (meaning I sit and work at the computer most of the day) I am too tired to exercise at night.

Find what you are most likely to do. The reality is that some people may not have a favorite sport or activity. This is an opportunity to explore what you will be able to incorporate into your daily life.

Pace yourself. Most of us can benefit from increasing the amount of time we do an activity. To do this in a way that is reasonable, start a new activity slowly, and over time increase your pace.

Know your healthy heart rate. Stay within a safe range. Talk to your health care provider about what is best for you to do.

We all need to keep at the forefront of our thoughts what is happening inside our bodies as well as the outside forces (culture and advertising) that drive us in the wrong direction. To make your journey easier it helps to keep what you do simple: eat healthy, remember that there are no forbidden foods, be as active as possible, and relish mild hunger.

[1] Harvey, E. L.; Summerbell, C. D.; Kirk, S. F. L. and Hill A. J. "Dietitians' Views of Overweight and Obese People and Reported Management Practices," *Journal of Human Nutrition and Dietetic,* October 2002, Volume 15, Issue 5, pages 331–347.

[2] Zhu, D.; Norman, I.J. and While, A. E. "The Relationship Between Health Professionals' Weight Status and Attitudes Towards Weight Management: A Systematic Review," *Obesity Reviews* 2011 May; 12(5):e324-37.

[3] Sacks, F. M.; Bray, G. A.; Carey, V. J.; Smith, S. R.; Ryan, D. H.; Anton, S. D.; McManus, K.; Champagne, C. M.; Bishop, L. M.; Laranjo, N.; Leboff, M. S.; Rood, J. C.; de Jonge, L.; Greenway, F. L.; Loria, C. M.; Obarzanek, E. and Williamson, D. A. "Comparison of Weight-Loss Diets with Different Compositions of Fat, Protein, and Carbohydrates," *The New England Journal of Medicine.* February 26, 2009, Vol. 360, No. 9, Pgs. 860-873.

[4] Gudzune, K.A.; Doshi, R. S.; Mehta, A.K.; Chaudhry, Z.W.; Jacobs, D.K.; Vakil, R. M.; Lee, C.J.; Bleich, S.N. and Clark, J.M. "Efficacy of Commercial Weight-Loss Programs: An Updated Systematic Review," *Annals Internal Medicine* 2015; 162:501-512. doi:10.7326/M14-2238.

[5] Reinhardt, M.; Thearle, M. S.; Ibrahim, M.; Hohenadel, M. G.; Bogardus, C.; Krakoff, J. and Votruba. S. B. "A Human Thrifty Phenotype Associated with Less Weight Loss During Caloric Restriction," *Diabetes.* Published ahead of print May 11, 2015. DOI: http://dx.doi.org/10.2337/db14-1881

[6] Rodriguez, J. C. *The Diet Selector.* Running Press. Philadelphia, 2007.

[7] Hall, K.A.; Bemis, T.; Brychta, R.; Chen, K. Y.; Courville, A.; Crayner, E. J.; Goodwin, S.; Guo, J.; Howard, L.; Knuth, N. D.;

Miller, B. V.; Prado, C. M.; Siervo, M.; Skarulis, M. C.; Walter, M.; Walter, P. J. and Yannai, L. "Calorie for Calorie, Dietary Fat Restriction Results in More Body Fat Loss than Carbohydrate Restriction in People with Obesity." *Cell Metabolism* 22, 1–10 Sept.1, 2015 a2015 Elsevier Inc. DOI: http://dx.doi.org/10.1016/j.cmet.2015.07.021

8   "Low-fat May Beat Low-Carb Diet for Trimming Body Fat: Study in Healthy Day News," MedlinePlus: Trusted Health Information for You. August 13, 2015.

9   Zeevi, D.; Korem, T.; Zmora, N.; Israeli. D.; Rothschild, D.; Weinberger, A.; Ben-Yacov, O.; Lador, D.; Avnit-Sagi, T.; Lotn-Pompan, M.; Suez, J. et al. "Personalized Nutrition by Prediction of Glycemic Responses." *Cell*. Volume 163, Issue 5, November 19, 2015, Pgs. 1079-1094 DOI: http://dx.doi.org/10.1016/j.cell.2015.11.001

10   Food and Drug Administration. "Questions and Answers on Dietary Supplement." 2015.

11   Starr, Ranjani. "Too little, too late: Ineffective Regulation of Dietary Supplements in the United States." *Public Health Ethics, American Journal of Public Health*. March 2015. Vol 105, No. 3.

12   Journal of the American Medical Association. "Presence of Banned Drugs in Dietary Supplements Following FDA Recalls." Research letter. October 22/29 2014.

13   Martin, C. K.; Church, T. S.; Thompson, A. M.; Earnest, C. P. and Blair, S. N. "Exercise Dose and Quality of Life: A Randomized Controlled Trial." *Archives of Internal Medicine*, Vol. 169, No. 3, February 9, 2009, Pgs. 269-278.

[14] White, J. and Jago, R. "Prospective Associations Between Physical Activity and Obesity Among Adolescent Girls: Racial Differences and Implications for Prevention," *Archives of Pediatric Adolescent Medicine*, Vol.L 166 (No. 6), June 2012. Pgs. 522-527.

[15] Chmelo, E. A.; Crotts, C.; Newman, J. C.; Brinkley, T. E.; Lyles, M. F.; Leng, X.; Marsh, A. P. and Nicklas, B.J. "Heterogeneity of Physical Function Responses to Exercise Training in Older Adults," *Journal of the American Geriatric Society*. 2015 Mar; 63(3):462-9.

[16] The National Center for Complementary and Integrative Health of the National Institutes of Health, August 2015.

CHAPTER 7
Know What You Are Doing

According to behavioral research, just measuring something changes it. In my case and in the case of many others, tracking weight, either formally or informally, was not enough to maintain the weight at the desired level. I have decades of weight charts. Obviously, tracking my weight, no matter how methodically, did not make it possible to maintain my healthy weight, even though I knew that it would be good for me. I had the practice of tracking, but it did not produce the desired outcome.

Most of us do track our weight either formally or informally. Almost all of us know how much we weigh, even though we may not tell others. Those of us who carry excess weight also have an idea of how much we would like to weigh. Some of us believe that we should weigh the same amount as we did in high school or college. Others focus on always being a specific clothing size, regardless of the huge variation that we know exists in clothing sizes. These types of goals are often a prescription for failure, since they do not take into account how our physical activity and wellness changes over time.

Translating all the research into how it applies to people made it clear that having an overly-ambitious goal would doom my effort to failure. The good news was that my goal no longer had to be attaining a weight that would put me in the normal range. It was okay, if not preferable, to be overweight. What I needed to know was how to translate this research into my life. In other words, how would I create a target that would get me to a healthier place and keep me there for the rest of my life?

The importance of tracking is that over time you will be able to see how far you have come in managing your weight. You will use the information to help you know what you are doing and when you may need to recalibrate your new ways of thinking and eating. You can do this in whatever manner works for you. The key aspect is to use the information that you collect to objectively inform yourself and to know what bolsters or undercuts your efforts.

Tracking Weight. I know you have probably weighed yourself so many times that you know how to stand, jiggle, and get on the scale to minimize your weight. But this is a life-long plan and not just a temporary part of your life. Put all you did in the past aside, and get in the practice of weighing yourself in the morning. It is good to weigh yourself, first thing in the morning, and without any clothes.

I used to travel a lot and would weigh myself as soon as I got home from a long flight. My weight would be up two to three pounds. A few days later I would weigh myself and celebrate that I had lost weight one to two pounds. In reality I had not lost any real weight and was in fact gaining weight.
—Harriet

Daily weigh-ins made me think about the connections between my activity, specific foods, and nutrients. I do not record my weight on a daily basis. I discovered that when I eat out, I may eat the same number of calories, but there is so much salt in the food that I end up weighing more than if I had eaten at home. Apparently the fact that I do not add salt to any of the tasty food I prepare at home changed how much water I retained. Daily weigh-ins are a guide as to how to rethink how I eat and move. I used weekly weigh-ins to track how I was doing overall. Wednesday is my weigh-and-record day.

Tracking clothing. Instead of focusing on a specific clothing size as my goal, I picked a couple of my "someday" clothes as my goal. I returned to them every few months.

After a few months of my weight coming down, I noticed that my pants were getting looser. A few months later, my standby pants were longer, and I had to roll up the waist. It took me a while to realize that the L. L. Bean pants that I had worn for decades were just too big for me. I was surprised to find that I had gone from a Petite XL to a Petite Large. Eventually I went to a Petite Medium. Clothes that had been in my "someday" section finally fit; eventually, some were even too big. Looking at myself in the mirror, I found that visually the shift had not been as dramatic as what I had seen in all those ads about weight loss. But the clothes provided the tangible evidence of how I changed my size.

Tools to Track Your Food and Activity. There are many apps and tools that you can use to capture your information on a regular basis. Some are free and some have a minimal cost. When it came to knowing how much I was actually eating and how much I was doing, I found MyFitnessPal.com to be the most helpful.

Using the site is free, and there is also an app that you can use on your other devices. Once you subscribe, you set your diet/profile setting by entering your current weight, height, your goal weight, gender, and date of birth. Your next step is to describe your normal daily activity. For most of us it would be safe to choose "sedentary," which means that you spend most of your day sitting. Indicating "sedentary" will also give you a conservative estimate of how much you need to eat on a daily basis. As part of your activities, you also have to indicate the frequency and length of time for your proposed workouts.

The next step is to decide your goal. Seven goals are listed:

- Lose 2 pounds per week
- Lose 1½ pounds per week
- Lose 1 pound per week
- Lose ½ pound per week
- Maintain my current weight
- Gain ½ pound per week
- Gain 1 pound per week

For those of us who want to lose weight, a goal of ½ pound per week is ambitious but reasonable. Based on your goal, your suggested fitness and nutrition goals are presented.

The next step is completing the check-in screen. This is where you can record your baseline weight and measurements. MyFitnessPal lets you choose what you want to measure and track. At the very least, you want to measure your waist size. I also measured my hips, bust, thigh (right), and arm (right), because I thought it might provide some insights on my progress. You can add other parts of your body too.

While I recorded my weight weekly on a piece of paper, I only entered my weight in MyFitnessPal every few weeks. I recorded the other measurements of my body even more sporadically. Still, it was good to have this information because I could use it as a gauge of where I was and where I am now.

The section on exercise provided very useful feedback on my movement. On those days that I exercised, and there were not as many as I would have wanted, I was able to record my exercises and see how many calories I actually expended. It was easy to do, because most cardiovascular and strength training activities are in their database. And while you have to enter your specific exercises the first time, the next time you want to add your activity, they will appear on your list.

All the information about movement was very motivating. I was pleased to see that my seventy-five minutes of shoveling snow used many calories. It became clear that even doing some mild stretches added to the calories I could eat for the day.

I also liked the fact that the MyFitnessPal app that I had loaded onto my phone was linked to a step counter that kept track of my activity. These results were then integrated with my food diary. Having the impact of the calories I ate and my exercising coordinated was very helpful. The more I walked, the more calories I could eat.

This is the easiest way to keep track of calories and nutrients. They have a huge database of the calories and nutrients in food from the grocery stores to the major chain restaurants. I was most delighted by the ability to import my recipes and have it calculate the calories. I was able to quickly calculate how many calories are in one of my servings of fishmonger's stew, pasta with garlic and anchovies, and paella. It was also fun to see how I could tweak my standard recipe to reduce the calories.

The reports section was helpful in visualizing the changes I had experienced. After a few months, I could see that my weight went down. But it was not a straight line down. The trend was more of a slow zigzag in the downward direction. There would be a few weeks when nothing would happen (zig), and then I would lose weight (zag). Then the process would start again. Over time, it seemed that vacations and festivities made the zig part longer before it would zag down. I would remind myself to focus on the downward trend. When I look at the chart of the last year, I am still amazed about all the weight I lost. You can produce all sorts of reports about the trends for your weight, nutrition (calories, carbohydrates, fats, protein, saturated fats, cholesterol, sodium, etc.), and fitness. You have to decide which reports will help you manage your weight.

There were parts of MyFitnessPal that I did not use. Blog posts from other users, forum topics, and their many tips were not of interest to me.

The food diary was the core of what I tried to record every day. I have to admit that for the first few weeks I just did rough calculations from my head. Once I started to measure and record regularly, I had a better sense of what I was eating. Since I was tracking calories, carbs, sodium, potassium, calcium, and iron, I could see the full value of each item I ate. That was important in helping me choose what I would eat and in understanding how what I ate could support or undermine the good practices that I was trying to make a part of my life.

I was impressed by how the people who developed MyFitnessPal made it clear that you have to eat a healthy amount of food. If at the end of day you ate too few calories for the day, MyFitnessPal would not let you know your projected weight if you continued to eat in that way. Instead, you would get a warning message that you were likely not eating enough, and that NIH recommends eating no fewer than 1,000 to 1,200 calories a day for women or 1,200 to1,500 calories for men. The message also pointed out that over time, not eating enough can lead to "nutrient deficiencies, unpleasant side effects, and other serious health problems." That is a key reminder, because sometimes people can be so focused on managing their weight that they forget that the goal is to be healthy. Managing your weight is a tool to help you be healthier, but it is not in and of itself sufficient for health or well-being.

It was sometimes amazing what I learned about myself from using MyFitnessPal. I was delighted when my friend Tassia invited us a barbecue to celebrate both the Fourth of July and her son's birthday. The bonus was that the meal would consist entirely of homemade Greek food. Trying to be thoughtful and plan in advance, I purposely ate less at breakfast so that I could enjoy the festivities and savor all of the tasty homemade food.

We were at Tassia's house from 1 to 6 pm. We talked, laughed, and enjoyed the feast. With the 3 Ps in mind, I purposely ate much less than what I wanted to eat and far less than I could fit into my stomach. I also drank only water, as I wanted to save my calories for the food.

The choices were so many, from moussaka to lamb to spanakopita. There were even several birthday cakes to satisfy a variety of food preferences. So I served myself a sliver—barely two tablespoons—of each cake. By the time we left, I felt somewhat full and knew that I would have at most a very light dinner.

By the time I got home I was curious as to how much I had actually eaten. I decided to calculate the calories in everything I ate, understanding that the estimates would be a little rough. I wanted to get an idea of how much I had eaten freely, without planning.

I used MyFitnessPal to get an idea of how many calories I had consumed. I was shocked at the total amount of calories. It was a whopping 2,164 calories (see below). I checked the projections for my calories and what it meant. The calculations were clear— if I ate like this every single day, in 5 weeks I would gain 11 pounds. In other words, it would take me only 5 *weeks* to gain back what I had lost over the last 5 *months*. That was shocking to me, and only reinforced what I knew. Keeping track of what I eat and how much I eat would have to be done on a daily basis. This was not a matter of choice, but an action that was essential to maintaining a healthy weight. I sighed to myself. Once again, life had reminded me that keeping weight off is a challenge.

1 p.m.	
Homemade spanakopita (5 triangles)	350
Greek salad side (very small)	38
2:30 p.m.	
Homemade moussaka (2 cups)	440
Grilled lamb chops (5 ounces)	330
Greek cheese pie (4 ounces)	275
Homemade spinach feta pie (1/2 wedge)	90
4:30 p.m.	
Generic baklava (2"x2")	418
Chocolate mousse cake (2 ounces)	223
Total	2,164

For me, tracking with MyFitnessPal was an essential tool to support all my new practices. There are many other apps for people who want to manage their weight.

For another friend, the structure and community of Weight Watchers provided what he needed. Moreover, there is considerable evidence that if you want to be a part of a group, Weight Watchers is the best program for you, especially given the reasonable costs. As in any group process, having a motivational group leader is essential. Foods are assigned food values, and each person is told how much they can eat. There are apps, online tools, books, and all types of supports. The Weight Watcher's program is about teaching you new practices about eating. As always, the struggle is to maintain the success you have achieved.

Track Your Overall Health. Your health care provider will be able to give you some information about how you are doing and any changes that they may have noticed.

This is your journey. So you are the best judge of how you are doing. Ask yourself, given where you started and all the work that you have done, how do you feel? Are there activities that you can do now that you could not do before? Are you able to do your favorite activities for longer? Will you continue on your journey?

This is a personalized plan that you have developed, fine-tuned and undertaken. The next steps are up to you.

EPILOGUE

The pioneer in obesity studies, Dr. Jules Hirsch, was a "physician-scientist. He helped reframe the modern understanding of obesity by demonstrating that people do not become fatter or thinner simply by indulging in or depriving themselves of food. His life's work supported biochemical explanations for a condition long attributed to personal weakness."[1] Dr. Hirsch's research documented that each person's body tended to get fixated on a certain weight regardless of whether or not that was the healthiest weight for the individual.[2] Over decades of research, he documented that some people were biologically predisposed to gain excess weight, and that the excess weight was probably caused by some disruption in the way the body converted what they ate into the energy needed.

As I was putting finishing touches on this book, I read Dr. Hirsch's obituary. He may not be as famous as all of the physicians and other health professionals who are associated with some revolutionary new way to lose weight, but in many ways he is an unsung hero. He documented the science that supported the claims of those of us who try to manage our weight. He showed that while getting to a desired weight is tough, staying at that weight is even tougher. This is not the quick and easy fix everyone is marketing. Dr. Hirsch is known to have said about losing weight, "They will feel miserable." But then he added, "But if they can do it, they will be better off."[3]

He was right. There were times when I did feel miserable. After all, we are trained that hunger is bad. And I had to learn how to eat enough to avoid headaches or being cranky. I had to teach myself that it was really okay to experience mild hunger. I learned to eat slower, so that my brain could register the fullness in my stomach. And I learned to wait a bit when I was hungry so I could appreciate and savor everything that I did eat.

I found that over time I was able to better navigate the rough waters that are part of staying at a healthier weight. I have no doubt that being thoughtful about what and when I eat will be with me for the rest of my life.

I still use MyFitnessPal to help me be aware of how much I am eating. I know that I have to use the information to help gauge my choices of food and activity. There are no forbidden foods, just foods I have to plan to eat (like pizza and ice cream). When I do just eat what I want because the food is so fabulous, I know that I will have to make up for it later.

It has been over two years since I started on this journey. Some days are harder than others, but knowing the benefits to my life has made all the difference.

---

1   Langer, Emily. "Jules Hirsch, Physician-scientist who Reframed Obesity, Dies at 88. Obituary," *Washington Post*, August 3, 2015.

2   Leibel, R.L.; Rosenbaum, M. and Hirsch, J. "Changes in Energy Expenditure Resulting from Altered Body Weight," *New England Journal of Medicine*. March 9, 1995. Vol. 332 Pgs. 621-628 DOI: 10.1056/NEJM199503093321001

3   Weber, Bruce. "Jules Hirsch, Pioneer in Obesity Studies, Is Dead at 88." *New York Times*, July 30, 2015. Page A16.

ACKNOWLEDGEMENTS

This book was written based on the hard earned knowledge and insights of the people who shared with me their experiences in improving their health by making changes in their life. In addition, there are some very special people who made this book possible.

First and foremost, I want to thank my mother Lucy who gave me the positive outlook in life that has sustained and nurtured in me a healthy self-image and a belief in all that is good and possible. My husband, Mark provided the love and support through the decades, as we went through the many changes that were part of our life and that are reflected in the pages of this book. He also was patient as I stayed up late working during weekends and vacations as I tried to fine tune this and every other book I have written.

Adolph, Cynthia, Tom, and Marti encouraged me at every turn and in every way possible. Keith, Ron, Helaine, Jim, and Donna provided the inside industry knowledge to publish this book even though it did not have the typical weight loss gimmick that attracts agents and publishers. When I was discouraged, Larry made me laugh with his description of his attempts to manage his weight including one that meant eating lots of cottage cheese (even cottage cheese with ketchup!). Larry also came up with the title for this book. Without Adolph's and Bill's guidance in navigating the new realities of publishing this book would never have been in print.

There are also wonderful people in my life who provide love, wisdom, and guidance; support my passions; and, temper my desires on an as need basis— Ileana, Kevin, Amanda, Sheila, Tatyana, Msgr. Duffy, Esther, Gladys, Carolyn, Roy, and Rosamaría. I also remember my Cousin Deborah and Henrietta.

I owe my deepest gratitude to all of these exceptional individuals and the many more I could not fit on these two pages. I want to thank them again for all they do and for all the inspiration and critiques they provide. I am deeply honored to have each one of them in my life.

INDEX

45456964R00099

Made in the USA
Middletown, DE
04 July 2017